ALSO BY JOHN P. DAVIDSON

*The Soul's Critical Path:*
*Waking Down to the Soul's Purpose,*
*the Body's Power, and the Heart's Passion*

*Soul Tribes & Tambos:*
*Communities for Souls on the Move*

*The Left Hand of God:*
*A Soul's Love Poems*

# BREAKING WITH BELIEF, RECLAIMING THE GARDEN

# BREAKING WITH BELIEF, RECLAIMING THE GARDEN

*Finding the Body, Heart, and Soul*
*of a Purposeful Spirituality*

John P. Davidson

HeartWorks
PUBLISHING

HeartWorks Publishing is a trademark of HeartWorks Publishing Company.

Cover Art: "Lilith in the Garden" Copyright Amy Rankin 1995
Cover Design: John P. Davidson
Interior Book Design: Booknook.biz

Davidson, John P. (John Philip), author.
Breaking with belief, reclaiming the garden : finding the body, heart, and soul of a purposeful spirituality / John P. Davidson.
pages cm
Includes bibliographical references.
ISBN 978-0-9973116-0-0

1. Soul. 2. Spirituality. 3. Evolutionary
psychology. 4. Consciousness. 5. Ethnobotany.
6. Ayahuasca. 7. Healing.  I. Title.

BL290.D378 2016      204
                QBI16-600042
Library of Congress Control Number: 2016903622

HeartWorks Publishing Company
P.O. Box 6
Raton, New Mexico USA 87740
www.heartworkspublishing.com

*For my daughter, Paige, who asked the right question*

*If you bring forth what is within you, what you bring forth*

*will save you. If you do not bring forth what is within you,*

*what you do not bring forth will destroy you.*

Gospel of Thomas

*(Trans. George MacRae[1])*


*Seeing, contrary to popular wisdom, isn't believing.*
*It's where belief stops, because it isn't needed anymore.*

*Terry Pratchett,*

Pyramids


*Many people can hold the parts, many people can hold*
*the whole, but very few people can hold*
*the parts and the whole.*

*Hugh Milne,*

The Heart of Listening

# CONTENTS

PROLOGUE

AUTHOR'S FOREWORD

INTRODUCTION          1

### PART ONE
### WHAT'S AT WORK: THE HUMAN TRINITY

INTRODUCTION TO PART ONE      13

CHAPTER 1

SOUL: CONSCIOUSNESS DISTILLED      19

*Soul as a Singular Sense*      24

*The Soul as Field*      27

*The Now of the Soul*      28

CHAPTER 2

BODY: CONSCIOUSNESS SENSUALIZED      29

*The Commonly Identified Senses*      30

*Analytic Understandings: Sensing Meaning*      31

*Vision: Sensing Relation*      31

*Emotions: Sensing Feelings*      32

*Gut: Sensing Danger*      33

*Intuition: The Subtle Sense*      33

*Other Aspects of the Body*      34

*Body as a Liquid Crystalline Structure*      34

*Personality*      35

*Desire*      37

*Life Force*      39

*The Body's Now*      40

CHAPTER 3

    HEART: CONSCIOUSNESS CONNECTED    43

        *The HeartMath Institute*    44

        *Mae-Wan Ho*    45

        *Joseph Chilton Pearce*    47

        *The Heart Portal*    48


PART TWO

HOW IT WORKS: THE TRILOGY OF HUMAN INTELLIGENCE

INTRODUCTION TO PART TWO    55

CHAPTER 4

    KNOWING: THE EXPERIENCE OF CONNECTION    61

        *Fishing*    61

        *Knowing as Raw Experience*    63

        *The Depth of Raw Experience*    65

CHAPTER 5

    THINKING: THE INTEGRATION OF EXPERIENCE    75

CHAPTER 6

    VISIONING: THE POSSIBILITY OF EXPERIENCE    85

CHAPTER 7

    EXPANDED THINKING AND VISIONING    91

        *The Mind's Eye*    91

        *The Mind's Ear*    93


PART THREE

WHAT RESISTS IT: BREAKING WITH BELIEF

INTRODUCTION TO PART THREE    99

        *Breaking with Belief*    99

        *Defining Belief*    100

        *Why We Rely on Belief*    101

The Error of Science      103

The Now Apparent Problem      105

CHAPTER 8

  THE GNOSTIC GOSPELS      109

CHAPTER 9

  THE EARLY YEARS OF CHRISTIANITY ACCORDING
  TO PAGELS      115

The Emergence of a New Community      115

The Competition for Control      117

St. Irenaeus      124

Constantine the Great      126

St. Augustine      128

CHAPTER 10

  A SPIRITUALITY WITHOUT BELIEF      133

The Question We Need to Ask      133

CHAPTER 11

  A DEFINING DIFFERENCE BETWEEN RELIGION
  AND SPIRITUALITY      149

Two Distinct Processes      149

The Evolution Toward Maturity      156

CHAPTER 12

  BELIEF'S EMPIRE AND THE ABSENCE OF EMPATHY      159

An Empire Built on Belief      159

An Absence of Empathy      165

The Teaching of Trees      173

PART FOUR

HOW TO WORK IT: A TR(ILOGY OF) ACTION = TRACTION

INTRODUCTION TO PART FOUR      179

Intention      180

Imagination      180

Attention      181

CHAPTER 13

    SHIFTING IDENTITY TO THE SOUL            183

       *How a Session Looks*            185

CHAPTER 14

    FROM SOUL RETRIEVAL TO BODY RETRIEVAL    199

       *Why We Heal*            199

       *What Healing Is*            200

       *Healing the Soul First*            202

       *Shifting Focus to the Body*            205

       *How We Invite and Integrate the Healing*            209

       *Journeying Outside the Body*            216

CHAPTER 15

    A ROLE FOR PLANT MEDICINES AND OTHER HEALERS    219

CHAPTER 16

    DISCOVERING SOUL PURPOSE            229

POSTSCRIPT            235

ACKNOWLEDGMENTS            241

APPENDIX            245

NOTES            255

ABOUT THE AUTHOR            259

# PROLOGUE

You say you have a dream.
I want to know if the dream has you.
Show me one priest
taken by Vision
who has not burned his Bible
and stripped his robe.
Or one rabbi
truly hearing even a single Word
who has not torn the Talmud
and raced from the temple.

Don't tell me what you believe,
or even what you think.
Tell me if dreaming wiped that mind aside
and showed soul
how to breathe your body.
Your little dreams,
those night and day dreams,
they have their use.
But give me waking visions.
I would have them pull me apart
and put me back together.

I have been to the Tree.
I have seen the Blessed Serpent.
My body was laid across the roots
and healed in sparkling brown mud.
And I was taken deep
into the Earth's own heart
more than once,
until *I* learned the way.
Little serpents carried me there,
rich earth brown and patterned serpents
and white serpents with rainbowed backs,
while my body dissolved into joy.
I saw Adam born
from the womb of my own body.
I watched *that* Adam find Eve
in the valley of the dying.
I watched the undermountain women heal Eve
and do the same for Adam.
*I am* that Adam
and my body that Eve,
as Earth is heaven's Eve.
And I have eaten the fruit of the Tree,
many times.
We are not banished from the Garden
but expanded,
exploded into interdimensional beings
while the Garden holds space
for our shining return,
brilliant little suns
rising upon Earth's horizon,
illuminating creation's path.

*Heart* is my temple.
Not the beating heart,
not the emotional heart,
nor the celebrated chakra,
but the Portal Heart,
the doorway *to* the body
through which soul whispers sweetness,
beckoning the body.

*Come my love*
sings the soul.
*I* am that soul.
And body turns to soul
when there is agony enough,
when the pain is so great
that body seeks soul's safe haven.
How blessed the paradox of being,
that persistent pain
will dog the body
into soul's loving arms,
when pain can finally turn the body
toward soul's healing sound,
so the work can begin.

# AUTHOR'S FOREWORD

## A Soul Perspective

EACH DAY, WE MAKE A CHOICE. Each day, we have the opportunity to choose a life of purpose. We have the opportunity to tune into the sense inherent to all humans that we are on the planet for an important reason. We have the opportunity to find within that sense the unique gift that each of us brings to the planet, and the opportunity to find a way to deliver that gift on this day in a way that did not exist yesterday. Choice opens a door. Walking through that door is also an *initiation*—an invitation to transformative experience. Purpose lies within that continual transformation.

For a very few, that choice seems easy to make. For many more of us, the opportunity to choose a purposeful life is overshadowed by our preoccupation with life's challenges. It is common to be carried along not by choices underwritten by a clear sense of purpose, but by the momentum of the body's survival instinct. It is common for many to persist in a sense of confusion about what their life means, even though some inkling of purpose may bubble up from time to time. For so many of us, the predominant sense is that life is a struggle.

And for a significant number of us, our daily choice is whether to continue the struggle or just give up the fight. For those, the instinct to survive, and perhaps fear of death, may be overcome by the sheer weight of a life that seems both purposeless and too much to bear.

Purpose and soul are inextricably linked. If you picked up this book, I suspect you already knew that. But what you may not know is that how we make the choice comes down to skill. It is a soul skill.

It is one thing to sense that you have a soul, to feel that your life has an important purpose, and to yearn for the revelation of that purpose.

It is another to understand how the expression of soul purpose is not predetermined, but co-created by a soul's unique gifts resonating with new possibilities continuously churned up by a rapidly changing world.

And it is another thing yet to understand how the process of creation itself depends absolutely upon the soul's skillful engagement of the body's incredibly diverse sensuality and potentially powerful life force. That greater understanding can be discovered by experiencing what the soul and body hold in common with the ever-changing world.

Humans live in a *coherent* world. In a general sense, "coherence" means that there exists a harmony among distinct parts doing their respective jobs as part of a greater whole. It implies correlation, a sticking together, connectedness, and a consistency in a systemic operation. Whether we recognize it or not, coherence cuts across all aspects of life, whether the harmonious parts make up a computer, a plan, an ant's body, an ecology, or the intelligent design of the cosmos.

Human bodies are designed to operate coherently. What little we know of our bodies reveals a harmonic synchronization at the level of electromagnetic communication that gives rise to the ability, for example, to play a musical instrument, digest dinner, express love, catch a fly ball, or solve problems. Yet most humans live in a state of incoherence, both internally and relative to their environment, because operating coherently in an increasingly chaotic world requires skill. Humans experience incoherence as a sense of disconnection.

The sense is accurate. Humans have now largely disconnected from nature. Close connection to nature provided both coherence and a sense of connection for humans throughout human history. Disconnection from nature became relatively complete in American culture as people moved from farms to towns and cities and, increasingly, indoors. Americans are perhaps the first culture to experiment so broadly with this literal disconnection from the earth. To its credit, that separation—and the exploitation of fossil fuels that accompanied and enabled this separation—has resulted in a radical leap forward in our standard of living and technological capabilities. But because of this abrupt separation from nature without a compensating skill of coherence, we have wound up in a dysfunctional relationship with the earth upon which we depend. Our move forward has come at great risk to our future on the planet. The experience of disconnection, arising from incoherence, underlies the pathologies of our time. Disconnection, and our inherent sense of it, is the root of our stress, disease, discontent, struggle, and inability to choose a life of purpose.

The ability of an individual human to reconnect with the earth and navigate the material world with soul purpose depends upon learning how to create coherence first within oneself and then with the coherent fields found in the world around us. While you do not need to have a scientific understanding of coherence to connect with your soul purpose, emergent research does offer some help in explaining how coherence is found by situating a self-identified soul in the heart. What *is* valuable to understand is that soul purpose and passion lie on that path of heart. Heart is not only the soul's gateway to a coherent relationship with the body, but also the connection to those coherent fields outside the body that guide the soul's way in the world. The creation of coherence and connection through the heart is a soul skill.

My work supports the development of such skill, including the ability to achieve the emotional healing that is coherence's first work in the body. The healing of which I speak is what the skillful soul alone can bring to the body. But, important as healing is to humans, healing is not an end in itself. There is a critical relationship between emotional healing and soul purpose.

Pain absorbs the body's sensory attention and holds it inward. Yet our ability to find resonance between soul purpose and the daily opportunities to enact our purpose in the world depends entirely upon our ability to turn attention to the world with all of the information-gathering ability of the body's extraordinary sensory capacity. Consequently, soul purpose can only be discovered and engaged when the senses of the body are no longer so preoccupied by pain. Pain also blocks the body's ability to draw in the planetary life force that is its birthright. So, healing the pain that absorbs our attention and minimizes our life force is critical, but still only an intermediary step in acquiring the ability to discover the purpose for which we have come to the planet.

But there is another aspect of pain that is commonly overlooked, even though occasionally acknowledged. Carl Jung famously said, "There is no coming to consciousness without pain." There is a special kind of pain that arises when the soul is suppressed and prevented from emergence by the unresolved traumas of our lives. That pain is the built-in signal that the soul is not only ready to emerge from its silent enmeshment with the body, but must emerge if sanity is to be maintained and soul purpose discovered (although soul purpose has certainly emerged in the midst of "insanity," but it isn't as much fun). The buried soul has the strength of the seed that will ultimately break the concrete of the sidewalk culture installed over it.

Long before Jung, the same message appeared in the Gospel of Thomas that was suppressed by the emergent Catholic Church and unearthed in the last century at Nag Hammadi: *If you bring forth what is within you, what you bring forth will save you. If you do not bring forth what is within you, what you do not bring forth will destroy you.*[1] It is the soul that must come forward to save us. It is the emergence of the soul that represents the level of healing that is tantamount to breaking the cultural cement that overlies our soul purpose. Nothing else will accomplish the healing that underwrites the emergence of soul purpose.

Even though none of us heals without at least some help from skilled practitioners, healing is ultimately something you have to accomplish yourself. Healing yourself is a soul skill, and finding purpose requires a soul skill enacted in collaboration with a healed body. If you want to experience the passion of your soul on fire with purpose grounded meaningfully on the planet, you'll want to develop these soul skills.

I teach how to focus the soul, ground it in the heart, and partner it with the body. When that partnering occurs, the body can find its place of safety with the soul, surrender to the work of healing, then place its physicality, desire, and life force in service of the soul's agenda. Then purpose can emerge concretely and dance competently with the external circumstances that spiral unpredictably but coherently around our lives.

I have written two earlier books about souls. In *The Soul's Critical Path: Waking Down to the Soul's Purpose, the Body's Power, and the Heart's Passion,* I described a way of understanding our spiritual journeys from a *soul perspective.* I suggested that souls have the capacity to evolve along a predictable pathway during a single lifetime of the body; that humans are on the planet to further the open-ended task of creation in the dimension of matter; that souls carry the imprint of unique gifts we bring to that task; that souls have the unique capacity to take primary responsibility for leading and guiding the healing that must happen before the body willingly provides legs for the soul's work; and that learning how to love and receive love are not simply important ends in themselves, but skills we have to learn to make our creations sustainable rather than destructive. This soul perspective represents a next stage in the evolution of human consciousness and, with that, a next step in the evolution of our healing modalities. For those readers who resonate with this message, I would recommend a reading of *The Soul's Critical Path,* but I have included for quicker reference an appendix that summarizes the stages of soul evolution I describe in that book.

In *Soul Tribes and Tambos: Communities for Souls on the Move,* I described a model for small communities that can provide a home for those young and mobile souls who are already consciously working to become skillful co-creators on the planet while looking for their tribes. I talked about how to fuse the technologies of meditative and indigenous traditions while cultivating a sustainable relationship with the earth.

In both of these books, I told the story of how my visions brought me to a direct experience of soul, helped to shift my identity from the body/mind/personality to the soul, and then informed the soul's own process of partnering with the body. I described some of those visions and their origins in daily meditations, meditation intensives in nature (sometimes called vision quests), shamanic journeys with the visionary plant medicines ayahuasca and huachuma (sometimes called San Pedro), and other spiritual initiations. In the midst of writing this book, I revisited the plant medicines in Peru and heard more information regarding our soul work on the planet.

My purpose in this book is to describe the efficient body of work that I have distilled from those experiences. I offer it as a practical process designed to ground your soul gifts in the work you came to do. Yet, as I was writing this book, I discovered that it was not enough to describe how soul and body work together. I realized the clients who come to me to learn this process were consistently hampered by the beliefs they held. I realized I was teaching a process that required dropping *all* beliefs in order to access the raw experience from which all knowing comes—including the insights that define soul purpose day by day. The process, I came to understand, required instead a curious and open mind, and the courage to explore and rely upon one's own experiences. My job was to show my clients a process by which they could touch directly into their own experience at the deep level that only a soul seated in the heart is able to achieve. That substitution of experience for belief, I came to understand, was a necessary condition of discovering soul purpose.

I saw how belief—both the *process* and a particularly toxic *content* of belief—had been interposed and then imposed upon Western thought by the emergent Catholic Church, then lost to our current understandings in the fog of history. I saw how the Church's story of our relationship to nature—our experience of the Garden—had warped our perceptions of ourselves and the world at a deeply unconscious level. I saw how science has paradoxically validated belief at the same time it joined with religion in invalidating personal experience. My experience with the plant medicines long used by some South American indigenous cultures gave me a distinctly different view of the human relationship to the gardened planet—one that is characterized not by a belief that humans are condemned to a life of suffering, but by the view that humans have the opportunity to co-create a sustainable way of being on a collaborative planet. In the space of vision that is the gift of a skilled soul perspective, one can discover how each of us is being called to reconnect, reclaim, and sustain—each in our own unique and purposeful way.

This book is about what I tell my clients. I say, I'm going to tell you a story. We use stories when we are dealing with mysteries beyond our ability to understand. The stories are bridges to experiences that will allow you to arrive at an understanding, not of the mystery, but of how to connect with mystery in order to engage collaboratively with it. You don't need to believe anything I say. We get into trouble when we believe our stories instead of recognizing them to be metaphoric means by which the mind can navigate what it can't understand. But, I tell them, you do need to set your own beliefs aside to get to an experience that those beliefs are blocking. *Try doing* what I say instead, I tell them. *Get a taste* of how it feels to experience your heart's knowing, free of the beliefs you've built up over time. If you get that taste, you'll have a start on how to find your own purpose within that vast mystery. Use this process until you find a better way to do it.

So my purpose in this book is not to tell you what your specific soul work is, but to show you a way to find it.

# BREAKING WITH BELIEF, RECLAIMING THE GARDEN

# INTRODUCTION

ON A VERY WARM NIGHT in November of 2000, I found myself lying face up on the hardened dirt floor of a circular ceremonial room in the small jungle town of Tarapoto, Peru. I was shirtless and barefoot, alternately chilling and sweating.

Along with some American companions, I had arrived earlier that day on a short flight from Lima. There had been just a little time to adjust to an entirely unfamiliar place and prepare for the first of the several ceremonies that were the object of our trip. Our expectations certainly included some measure of the healing for which ayahuasca has gained a considerable reputation and following. After sunset, prepared or not, we followed our shaman into his cement-block *maloka,* the common Peruvian name for jungle ceremonial structures, traditional and non-traditional alike. Shortly after dark, I swallowed a small cup of *ayahuasca,* given to each of us in turn by the shaman.

Ayahuasca is a bitter, thick brown tea made by boiling the ayahuasca vine and leaves of the chacruna or huambisa plant together for several hours. The mixture has come to be called an entheogenic or visionary plant medicine. The word "ayahuasca" itself translates as "vine of the soul" or "vine of death." In this context, "death" refers to the dying of our old identities as a new self emerges from this extraordinary experience.

There are several such natural medicines that bring a feast of otherworldly interactions by pushing our ordinary brain filters temporarily to the side. These medicines are sometimes called *master teaching plants.* One view of which plants are in that category would include not only ayahuasca, but also huachuma, peyote, jungle tobacco (sometimes called *mapacho*), psilocybin, iboga, and datura. Each has its own traditional use for healing and its distinct challenges.

As we settled in, the shaman sang softly, inviting the spirit of ayahuasca to join us. The shaman's songs, known as *icaros,* were simple, rhythmic prayers sung primarily in Spanish. At times, the songs were accompanied by soft drumming or rattling. Within less than an hour, the medicine began to take effect. The first sign of its action was a rigorous purging of the contents of my stomach—an almost universal effect of the ayahuasca. The purging not only empties the stomach, but is felt to empty the body of its unconsciously held traumatic memories. Diarrhea, also a form of purging, is a common result of drinking the ayahuasca as well.

The next effect of the medicine came with a small shock. I seemed to awake from a short slumber, finding myself floating above the street by which we had arrived earlier in the day. I was at the approximate elevation of the streetlight on the corner where our street joined a cross street. Drifting past the light, I turned the corner onto the cross street. The scene was unfamiliar since we had come to the shaman's center from the opposite direction. After floating a few more meters, I saw a health clinic, identifying it by the sign illuminated by the streetlight. Only in that moment did I realize I was not in the maloka. The thought arose that I should be. With that thought, I returned instantly to my still supine body. The next morning, I walked to the street and around the corner, finding the clinic just as I had seen it the night before. That experience had its own clear message: consciousness can travel outside the body.

Back in my body, I began to experience what would become a series of scenes that made up a waking vision. It did not matter whether my eyes were open or shut. I was seeing the same scene either way. In that part of the vision relevant to the theme of this book, I gave birth to a field of brilliant golden light that assumed the shape and size of a grown man. The luminous figure stood up and faced me briefly, then disappeared into my chest. During this part of the ceremony, my body felt completely held, safe, ecstatic, and connected. Words cannot, of course, fully convey the sense of the experience. There were many other new and extraordinary experiences that evening and during the ceremonies that occurred over the next several days. Throughout those ceremonies, the deep sense of connection never left. And the worldview I had held as I arrived in Peru was now hopelessly shattered. Its departure, in light of the new sense of connection, left me with no distress, but with a deep need to patch together a new way of seeing the world.

A few months after returning to the United States, I commenced a study of shamanism with an American teacher. In 2003, during a deathbed psychodrama that was part of this teacher's curriculum, I had a virtual near-death experience in which my consciousness entirely left my body for several minutes. During that journey out of body, I experienced a vision of visiting another dimension that I sensed as *home*. Again, I felt completely held, safe, ecstatic, and connected.

Several months later, while I was studying the death and dying process with Roshi Joan Halifax at Upaya Zen Center, she mentioned the HeartMath Institute and its research on heart-centered meditation. In 2004, I traveled to California to train at the Institute. As a consequence of that training, I shifted my daily meditation practice to include holding attention in my heart. I couldn't say then what in me had resonated with Roshi Halifax's mention of HeartMath or how it would connect with my jungle vision, but I *knew* that it would be important to investigate.

It would be more than ten years later, and many plant medicine ceremonies following that first ceremony, that a greater understanding of my first ayahuasca ceremony arose, one that would connect the dots of these experiences in a more comprehensive fashion than I could comprehend along the way. After the first ceremony in 2000, I continued to travel to Peru annually, in part to continue the connection with the spiritual teachings of that culture, but also because I began to be fascinated with how different that culture is from American culture.

In 2011, I began to recognize the experience of the golden field of light as a vision of my soul taking up residence in my heart, at least for that moment. I say "for that moment" because it had taken years for me to actually experience my soul as a distinct entity. It was a separate step yet for it to make its home away from home in my heart, and another step for me to sense that my identity had transferred to that being.

I told a more expanded story of my experiences, of which these were only a small part, in *The Soul's Critical Path*. In retrospect, connecting the dots has meant forming a more comprehensive but still provisional understanding that has formed around an understanding of soul, body, and heart as the critical players in the unfolding of human consciousness and planetary action.

While that understanding was forming, and during my travels to Peru and elsewhere, I encountered many young people. Listening to them, I developed a strong sense that old souls are crowding onto the planet just as the prospects for humanity's survival are reaching a critical juncture. Though most humans were born forgetting they came as souls, many of these young people have not forgotten.

These young people also expressed a definite sense of purpose. But our conversations made it apparent that the presence of even a strong sense that they came for a particular purpose does not define what the purpose is or how to ground it on a rapidly changing planet amidst an older generation seemingly bent on self-destruction. While many of these young people left home to hunt for tribe and purpose, they found rather quickly that the discovery of meaningful work at the level of soul purpose is not easy. Many of these gifted young people are having difficulty getting *traction*—getting soul purpose to work on the planet with the sense of passion that arises when you figure out how to do that.

In my conversations with them, I saw a connection between their challenge and the personal work that has emerged from my own soul journey. *I coach souls*—a distinctly different process than coaching a personal identity based in the sense that you are a body with a personality around which a benevolent if somewhat disconnected soul orbits. Coaching the soul is not about sorting through stressful and chaotic thoughts with the use of stress management techniques and talk therapy in order to make more rational choices. Soul work happens in the soul's connection with the body and world through the heart. Soul work does not happen first in the brain-mind. On the contrary, it requires overcoming the cultural implants that characterize the brain-mind's perspective. The cultural implants of which I speak are *beliefs*. I found it was necessary to break with belief altogether—not just the *content* of particular beliefs, but *the process of belief* itself.

Most of my coaching clients are middle-aged or older. They are people who have pursued a spiritual path for many years and come to me with at least some discipline of practice. Each has achieved some success and stability in the world long before they come to me. They come because they feel blocked in developing a clear sense of soul purpose fueled by the passion that accompanies the emergence of soul work. Their souls are also having traction issues, and part of those issues comes from their relationship with the process of belief itself.

Like the young people I have met, my clients yearn for a clearly defined purpose but don't know how to find it. Both groups have worked to make their bodies healthy and spirits strong, but they remain in uncomfortable relationship with them. Both experience a sense of disconnection that often gives rise to a degree of depression. For some, the degree of disconnection rises to the level to which we have applied the emergent diagnosis of PTSD. All my clients carry the emotional injuries of early psychological trauma that conventional psychological and alternative therapies have not healed. Still, all have gifts to share. All have lived through an extraordinary transformation of culture by technology and science that was unknown to humans only two generations ago. And all of them have a sense of the quickening—an urgency felt by many of us to search out opportunities for real soul work as the many crises that are causing broad environmental changes move inexorably closer to stopping us in our tracks.

No doubt, we have to move quickly. Fortunately, we have powerful tools at our disposal if we are willing to take responsibility for understanding how to use them. Western culture has become the beneficiary of a smorgasbord of spiritual traditions and therapeutic modalities from which we can pick and choose, allowing us to take what is valuable and leave behind what does not serve, at least if we choose skillfully. Classical spiritual traditions have certain inherent limitations that reflect perspectives acquired at earlier times in human evolution when life was slower and grounding on the planet was simpler. Those traditions also contain insights, techniques, and strengths we need to quickly adapt to our journeys. And mixed with the gifts those traditions hold is a process of belief that limits our effective use of those gifts.

Don Umberto Sancco Quispe—currently the spiritual leader of the Q'ero Nation of southern Peru—speaking to a small gathering in Peru in 2004, said that Westerners need to learn their traditions and "mix, match, and evolve" them. *Evolve traditions.* It is necessary, he says, not only to evolve ourselves, but to evolve traditions. Because time is no longer our friend, we have to learn how to go deeply within far more quickly than older cultures for whom time was ample and the support of nature more easily available. We need to search now beyond the goals of traditional spiritual perspectives. We are entering a different stage of human evolution, with a different goal that is closer yet to our ultimate purpose. Ascension to a sense of oneness was a primary goal of Asian spiritual culture. Now, descension to functional relationship with the planet and each other is a necessary goal of not only spiritual culture but human culture in general. While belief may have aided in the ascension, it will not be your friend in the descension. Not all of us will make that turn back to earth. But perhaps you are ready.

Modern therapeutic methods are giving new attention to the pathology of modernity: *disconnection* from family, community, tribe, earth, and self. We are developing a clear sense that humans suffer in general from an underlying sense of disconnection that feeds into all our other sufferings and ailments. We can easily see now that spiritual or psychic disconnection bleeds into physical disorders. Increasingly, we recognize that we need to experience connection to self, each other, and the whole. We understand that we need to love ourselves, each other, and the earth, and receive the love that is abundantly available to us.

But we lack a good understanding of how such a sense of connection arises. What connects with what? What does it mean to love one's self? What in us loves something else in us? Even if we believe that everything is connected, that belief doesn't translate directly to the *experience* of connection. Because our culture is busily creating disconnections, our compensating spiritual work is indeed about finding the experience of connection, at least as an initial step toward the deeper work. We are making progress in sorting this out, but despite millennia of human effort, we have only really started.

There is an evolutionary force at work that offers to speed that spiritual process. In the 1960s, mind-altering substances re-entered human consciousness after at least two millennia of religious and political suppression. Many who experienced LSD and psilocybin in the '60s discovered some sense of the underlying connection between humans and all else that exists. Because of countervailing forces in the national consciousness, that summering of a warmer, more connective consciousness faded into a fall harvest that reaped, instead, the material benefits of a booming economy. That prosperity facilitated for some a winter of withdrawal into the inner: a new period of self-reflection with meditation, yoga, chi gong, spiritual pilgrimages, and other consciousness-expanding techniques. Now, that winter is giving way to a new generational spring, coming with a renewed embrace of mind-altering substances, but with the significant introduction of additional entheogenic plants long honored by their use in indigenous traditions.

Medicinal science is not ignoring this emergence of plant medicines and their synthetic cousins. Psilocybin, LSD, MDMA, marijuana, and ayahuasca have become the subject of study for patients, including dying patients, for whom common pharmaceuticals offer neither healing nor a sense of connection, though those studies are narrowly limited. The lost sense of connection has become an increasing focus of our understanding of what we are calling PTSD. We are seeing this diagnosis applied not only to war veterans, but to abused women and others as we gain a better understanding of the effects of stress upon humans of all ages. One such understanding is that the head cannot cure the body without the body itself having the experience of connection that gives rise to a sense of safety. As we have searched for solutions, there is a growing awareness that the experience of connection is available, at least temporarily, from substances drawn directly from or modeled upon the molecular structure of particular plants still in use in indigenous cultures, as well as from nature, particular forms of meditation, and skillfully supportive relationships.

My own experience with a sense of disconnection giving way to a sense of connection has evolved over almost forty years of spiritual work. The evolution of that work ultimately came from a fusion within my own practice of two prominent spiritual traditions. Asia has taught us how to control attention. Indigenous shamanism has pointed that attention to the soul, the body, and the earth. The entheogenic plant medicines have given us the opportunity to experience the sense of connection within our souls and bodies deeply and quickly. With the fusion of Asian meditative practice and indigenous perspectives, there is an entirely new and more powerful possibility for humans. In this direction lies our evolution. That was a central message of *The Soul's Critical Path*.

That new direction is visible in the combination of several distinct elements: the ability to control attention (taught by Eastern traditions); the redirection of that skilled attention toward the body and earth (taught by indigenous traditions); the new understanding of coherence as the mechanism of connection that can be intentionally and skillfully cultivated (found in the work of a handful of scientists explaining an ancient understanding of that form of intelligence I will call *knowing*); a shift of personal identity from the body/mind/personality to the soul itself (also recovering what may be an ancient perspective); and a mentoring that teaches how to bring these elements together with direct experience through a process of preparation, support, and integration (what I provide with a process I call soul coaching*)*.

None of us do this alone. We all stand on the shoulders of our ancestors and all our relations. Still, we live in a new world with new potentials and time constraints. We are called upon to find new and efficient ways of becoming who we are on a planet that awaits our becoming capable partners in the open-ended process of creation—one soul at a time. Within this combination of elements lies the opportunity to break from belief and get some traction for our soul's purpose.

In this book, I want to present a three-part process alongside a fresh way of understanding our own three parts—body, heart, and soul—a trinity of collaborators that has the potential to bring traction to our soul purpose on the planet. The recognition of these elements is certainly not new. My work is a re-juxtaposition of these elements that provides a simple understanding amidst a complexity of available spiritual pathways, while recognizing that simple doesn't mean easy, even if simple may offer faster.

In Part One, I describe *what's at work* beneath the process of discovering soul purpose, which is a construct that defines soul, heart, and body as the three elements of a collaborative team. Part Two describes *how it works* by means of three intelligences I identify as knowing, thinking, and visioning. Part Three describes *what resists it,* in which I argue a radical position—that the process of belief completely interferes with our finding soul purpose. Lastly, in Part Four, I describe the three-part process itself—*how to work it.* This process requires skill development that allows us to shift personal identity to the soul, retrieve the body from the effects of its historic trauma, and use the sensuality of the body to discover and ground the soul's purpose moment to moment in meaningful work on a rapidly changing planet with the skill of coherence.

I do not intend a scholarly or scientific presentation, though what I present can find some support in both. Nothing I present here requires or requests belief; spiritual work not only does not require belief, but is effectively blocked by it. I rely on my own knowings and understandings from personal experience and will direct you to explore and rely on your own experience. Your heart will know whether there is resonance in what I have to say. Your mind will be unable to assess it unless you are willing to develop sufficient skill to experience this process on your own. My coaching offers an experiential and introductory taste. This book outlines the elements of that process and the grounded soul journey that can follow.

PART ONE

# WHAT'S AT WORK: THE HUMAN TRINITY

# INTRODUCTION TO
# PART ONE

PART ONE OFFERS MY CONSTRUCT about souls, bodies, and hearts.

A construct is an understanding. Understandings are definitional. Definitions are how we ascribe meaning in such a way that we can communicate with others with language. Constructs are never true, meaning that they are not a substitute for direct experience, even if they are useful in finding our way to the experiences that are the direct means for our journeys to unfold.

Whenever we approach a new subject or experience, we almost always, but not inescapably, do so with a construct already in mind. We carry understandings that we have accumulated over time. Whatever we have experienced in life, we interpret those experiences into understandings. These pre-existing understandings become, relative to new experiences, preconceptions that act like filters relative to the experience we are about to have. Those filters form expectations that pre-interpret new experience even before we can begin to taste it. They can block our ability to have an entirely new experience.

Even if we intend to approach what is new with a "beginner's mind," we seldom really do that, because doing so requires more than intention. It requires skill that few people have cultivated. It requires not only that we are able to control our precious attention but that we know exactly how to locate that attention within the field of our intelligences where raw experience is unimpeded by expectation. One can argue whether it is possible to have such a raw experience. I would argue that we can come much closer than we typically do if we develop the skills I describe in this book.

I would imagine that anyone reading this book is sympathetic to the idea that souls exist. Otherwise, you would not have picked it up and read this far. You have some ideas about souls. Those ideas are part of your filter.

What I offer here is likely a different filter about souls and soul purpose than the one you carry, but a temporary one nevertheless. I certainly don't ask that you *believe* what I say in this book, which would presume not only that my filter is better than yours, but that it is ultimately and undeniably true and universally helpful. I don't think that and certainly don't believe it. I try never to believe what I think. Belief is itself not only a powerful filter, but a dangerous one. I'll address specifically what I mean about belief in Part Three.

Instead, I suggest that you read what I have to say with a question in mind: Do you *resonate* with what I say from your own existing experience, which includes the intuition that arises within you from some source other than your thinking mind? If you do, then I suggest that you substitute the filter of my construct for your filters long enough to have a new and different experience of "soul," after which you can dispose of both your filter and mine and go forward with your new and deepening experience, which will give rise to your own new understandings.

So often, when we listen to the ideas of a writer or workshop presenter, we feel that we already know what they are saying, particularly if we resonate with what is being said. P. D. Ouspensky once complained that the greatest difficulty he had in communicating his ideas to audiences was getting across the message that what he had to say was actually different than what his audiences already knew and that his ideas were not just common information better communicated or more simply organized. Having spent forty years working on an eclectic spiritual path with many teachers, and with some diligent spiritual practitioners as clients, I say that what I have to say here is different. Perhaps it is new. Perhaps it is, after all, only old information more simply organized and more accessible to a modern audience. But I think it is not a common view. Please hold those possibilities in mind, and let your filter soften.

This may seem an overly self-conscious way to begin, but I want to emphasize what I will detail throughout the book: soul work begins with dropping understandings in order to get to direct experience. That experience may or may not ultimately be translated into understandings that can be communicated, but raw experience will certainly offer the mind the opportunity to form new understandings arising directly from your own experience. Soul purpose cannot be found elsewhere.

I will begin with the end of my story, which is my understanding of my experience. From there, I will work my way to what has become the true beginning of my story—a story about the process by which I came to the experiences of connection, the knowing that I am a soul, a functional relationship between myself and the body, and a sense of soul purpose and passion. My understandings are merely a bridge which, once crossed by you, need not be crossed again as you move into your own experience more deeply. These are bridges you can burn. In the native language of Peru, the teachers who embody such teachings are called *chakarunas,* a word for "bridge." We need not burn our teachers, but we do need to move on after their interpretations have taken us to our own deeper experiences. We need to become our own teachers, our own gurus. It is the experience, not the teacher, that will ultimately be of value to you.

An understanding, as I will detail in Part Two, is made of thinking. In Western culture, we are encouraged early on by our educational system to develop critical-thinking skills, just as we are encouraged by religion and politics to rely on belief. By both omission and shaming, we are also taught not to rely on our own capacity for knowing and visioning. To be sure, the human capacity for thinking is one beautiful expression of our distinctly human forms of intelligence. Thinking is critically important to our survival and evolution. But humans have other forms of intelligence—visioning and knowing. Culture does not encourage our developing these intelligences because culture is attached to thinking, scientific method, and belief. I say that the ultimate value of thinking depends upon its collaboration with visioning and knowing and upon our willingness to break with belief.

Because of our attachment to thinking, even by people who don't think of themselves as "thinkers," we tend to approach new experience from within a box called "thinking." Even those of you who lead with emotion are thinkers. And for all thinkers, all thinking is deeply colored with the emotion that is the body's memory of prior experience triggered by present events. One of my teachers liked to say that we can't think outside the box when the box is made of thinking. I'll add that the box is made not only of thinking, but of emotional reaction and belief.

What follows is an invitation to move outside that box and to contemplate that we can navigate the world effectively only by using all of our intelligences in a skillfully choreographed dance. We start to learn that dance by softening our attachment to thinking as the only important form of intelligence and to rationality and scientific method as the only useful forms of thinking.

The form of this invitation will come in my own truth, which is not factual. It is true only for me, and only because I have experienced it. It is not factual, because "facts" are a category reserved for identification of experiences reliably replicable by scientific methods of observation of the material world, a process conventional science advertises as "objectivity." The quantum physics view is trending toward an abandonment of the view that objectivity is possible. Either way, my personal and internal experiences are replicable only by me, and sometimes not even by me. Internal experience is the *only* way we can experience souls. Consequently, the understandings I have attached to my soul experiences are expressed in language that will not mean even approximately the same thing to someone who has not shared a similar experience. But, if my experience is genuine, you will recognize the truth of it in your own internal experience, even if the understandings that you draw from your experience are different. Truth resonates with truth, and all truths are inherently both personal and universal, even though understandings are not.

My soul construct is the best way my mind can assemble an understanding that is susceptible of communication. While I speak of *soul, body,* and *heart*—all familiar words—I know that these concepts might be expressed in the language of quantum physics: *fields, entanglement, toroids, coherence, non-equilibrium thermodynamics,* and so on. Both languages are essentially metaphors for experience. I will do some mixing of these metaphors. Bottom line, however—the language of my understandings comes from searching the literature for language to express my own experience that came in knowings and visions that required me to jettison prior understandings. I had to recognize that understandings that arise from our own experience, on the one hand, and beliefs that do not arise from personal experience, on the other hand, are incompatible. As I will explain in Part Three, such belief only mimics thinking and understandings. Belief is an inflexible filter that blocks the personal experience upon which our discovery of soul purpose depends. It is toxic to our intelligence. And it is addictive, like any other activity or substance we use to compensate for our sense of disconnection.

The construct I offer in Part One is a *soul perspective.* It is an understanding crafted from an experience as seen through the eyes of the soul peering through the sensory lenses of the body. I'll begin with an understanding that I will call *the human trinity* of soul, body, and heart—a construct I have found more sensible and helpful than the long-held trinity of body, mind, and spirit.

# I

# SOUL: CONSCIOUSNESS DISTILLED

HUMANS ARE A COLLABORATION of two very distinct and mysterious *entities*—*soul* and *body*—joined together by a third mystery commonly called *heart*. It's also possible to think of soul, body, and heart as three distinct *processes* that have the capacity to work together due to the underlying universal process of *coherence*. The human mind need not, and probably cannot, fully understand any of these processes, but we can *know and envision* them. The minimum we do need to understand is that these processes represent a potential and collaborative relationship that does not arise automatically but must be skillfully developed. Understanding the possibilities of that relationship and activating it skillfully allow us to make our soul journeys on the planet more efficient and effective.

To begin, we need to understand what part of this trilogy we are. The simple label "human" does not answer the question "Who am I?" in an effective way. For me, the sole answer to that question has become "I am the soul." I am the soul *part* of that collaboration. I am not the body part of that collaboration. I am not the heart part of that collaboration. Still, there is another "I," the I projected by the personality that is what the collaboration or its absence presents to the world—what the world sees as me.

That I includes not only the influence of a soul, but the influence of the body and the presence or absence of an operating heart.

These distinctions are critically important. The critical distinction is one of identity. Am I the I of the soul or the I of the body/mind/personality? Confusion about identity is at the very root of the human pathology of disconnection that is the root of human suffering.

My first book, *The Soul's Critical Path,* described in detail the experiences through which I came over many years to see the soul as who I am. Those experiences allowed me to form an understanding that the soul is quite distinct from the body and personality with which we most commonly identify. It is a different understanding than the common meditation perspective that *dis*-identifies with the body. A practice that simply negates body identity—*I am not the body*—but does not assume an alternative identity leaves us without identity. The complexity of Vedic, Buddhist, and Yoga traditions that would either deny individual identity as real or point to only a non-individual identity as real creates an understanding that—though not inherently untrue—makes it very difficult to find our way to individual purpose. In other words, the tendency of these popular Asian understandings as they have been presented to Western culture is to point our attention to oneness beyond the body, rather than to point our attention to an individualized soul consciousness that can learn to connect with an earth-based body that is, in turn, the pathway to purpose and creation.

Without belaboring this analysis, I will simply state that my understanding acknowledges the merger of human consciousness with the ultimate One only as an intermediate step on a journey that positions our souls for a skillful planetary journey of purposeful creativity. The soul, in this understanding, is the distillation of that universal oneness into a singular point of self-conscious awareness that can be skillfully placed within the heart of the body.

Looking at my journey in retrospect has allowed me to see how I could have moved forward much more quickly if I had seen that the ultimate goal is to be on the planet with purpose rather than to escape the challenges of planetary experience by holding my attention in the oneness. With that preliminary understanding, I could have applied the process directly, instead of discovering it slowly by trial and error in the midst of the beautiful and important Asian traditions that represent only an earlier stage in the evolution of human consciousness. At the same time, I sense that Buddhism is itself evolving toward a more active engagement of the body and the planet. The tradition is evolving.

With the emergence of a sense of soul distinct from a separate sense of body, I was eventually able to address body as an entity in its own right, with its own extraordinary powers and dignity. It is not necessary, I discovered, to fully understand the mystery of either soul or body to experience and understand that this distinction exists. As I sensed the soul as independent of my body, I began to see that it has a different function than that of the body. Giving that sensed function a name—*soul*—provides the mind with an abstraction that allows me to *think* about the experience. However, recognizing that any understanding arising from an encounter with the mystery of our being is never more than a provisional and inherently incomplete way to think about any such experience, my thinking has come to a softer quality. My commitment to think softly comes from recognizing that thinking tends to reify what is a moving, living encounter with a vast mystery into a "thing." Softening the propensity of the mind to objectify reality by naming it allows it to play with the vast mystery of reality in other ways, including knowing and visioning. Yet naming remains central to critical thinking.

So the thinking I have inferred from my experience goes this way. Soul comes from a dimension distinct from the dimension of time and space. Its nature seems timeless. It has no physical form other than the most subtle and singular of vibrations, but makes itself felt within the physical plane of time and space by means of a mystery I will call the "heart," the "portal heart," or the "heart portal." Being outside of time and space, the soul would seem infinite, or at least infinitely more expansive than a single lifetime of the body. It is of the nature of the One, but nevertheless, a singular distillation of It.

You might find it helpful to understand this soul to be like a radio wave that operates on a single frequency. Like a radio wave, the soul is a carrier frequency, meaning that it is encoded with information. I can tune my NPR station to that singular frequency on the FM band at 91.7hertz. But that carrier frequency is encoded with the vast range of additional frequencies represented by voice, music, and other sounds.

In the same way, the single frequency that represents your soul's location on an infinite frequency band of which it is a part also carries the variety of frequencies that encode the particular information that defines the soul's gift. And that gift defines the *potential* of your soul purpose. How we define the *actualization* of soul purpose is a function of learning the skill of bringing the soul's focused awareness into a very particular relationship with the body. When soul is in the body, the body lends a sense to the soul that lets the soul sense its own purpose in the moment—a moment that is defined by both the presence of a focused soul and an indeterminate flow of events in the world to which the body's sensuality gives the soul access.

For the moment, then, my suggestion is that you begin with the contemplation of the possibility that you are a soul, rather than a body/mind/personality with a soul orbiting somewhere far or near, and that the soul that you are is represented by a signature frequency that defines your nature and the gift you brought to the planet.

If you are an advanced practitioner of one of the Asian traditions, your existing filter may suggest that neither body nor soul is ultimately real. To those meditators, I would suggest that you contemplate that body and soul are both real, though differently real than the ultimate reality of which both body and soul are an emanation, and that body and soul have a purpose beyond being the unfortunate vehicles of suffering and ignorance from which we need to seek liberation. This may require, if you are a Buddhist practitioner capable of generating compassion, that you contemplate that engaged Buddhism is itself a way of turning the experience of the One back in the direction of the planet for a *planetary purpose* that is greater even than the exemplary goal of alleviating suffering. There is a greater potential purpose for a heart-centered focus than even compassion, and that greater purpose has to do with the manifestation of individual purpose in the service of co-creation of the cosmos.

If you are a Zen practitioner, you might contemplate that the practice of not naming might constitute an abdication of the potential of mind—acting with other powerful tools of human intelligences—to play its role in the process by which humans co-create the universe. Naming can be done softly, without the downfall brought on by complete reification. Just saying.

Experienced meditators will likely accept the idea that you cannot understand the ultimate reality, whether it is called Brahman, God, the Ultimate, or any of the ten thousand domain names already reserved. And many meditators accept the idea, or understanding, that you can *know* or *experience* that ultimate reality. I say to those meditators that the process by which humans have gained conscious access to that ultimate experience has often been fused with a belief that only that ultimate reality is real and that the earthly existence is somehow less real, or not real, or not as important as a re-mergence with the Ultimate. That filter, by focusing on an experience of the ultimate as the ultimate goal, causes us not to place the same degree of skillful attention on the body and soul, which, in my construct, are equally real and mysterious. We can know that the Ultimate exists, the body exists, the soul exists, and purpose exists, even if we don't understand why or how.

I know these statements are controversial and likely to put off many longtime meditators, but I would suggest some reasons to get beyond that reaction. First, the filters that traditional meditators use direct attention away from body for the most part, except in the service of bringing our attention to the oneness. Second, the experience of the oneness is so compelling that it is tempting to continue to orient in that direction, which is away from body. We have been conditioned by this traditional filter and the experience of oneness to see suffering as having no planetary purpose other than as motivation to merge with the oneness. Without our dropping that filter, we have little motivation to return to the suffering and to enter into it deeply enough to find how it reveals the soul's purpose on the planet. Without returning our attention to the sources of suffering as the pathway to soul purpose, we won't find it.

So I return to my original suggestion that you need to drop all of your filters, including the valuable and respectable filters that have brought us to meditation as we have known it, so that we can discover meditation as we don't know it. You can drop filters without dropping the experiences you have already gained. How to include and transcend skilled practices limited to the goals of liberation and the compassionate alleviation of human suffering, while further evolving your consciousness toward the skill of creative expression of individual purpose, is the subject of Part Four.

## Soul as a Singular Sense

Unlike the body, the soul has only a single sense, but it is the all-encompassing sense we call *consciousness,* or *awareness.* When that sense becomes focused, we call it *attention.* When I speak of soul, I refer to an entity that is distinct to itself but that may be anywhere on a continuum from unfocused and unaware of what it is to very focused and self-identified as the soul. This soul, at any point on such a continuum, provides the awareness sense that animates the body's multiplicity of senses. For purposes of being on the planet, that soul consciousness can't do much work without the body's more specialized senses. These specialized senses form the bridge between the pure consciousness of oneness and the experience of being on the planet. The body is the soul's hitchhiking guide to the earth.

This is why collaboration is necessary. Soul sense, in the form of generalized consciousness, needs the body's senses, in the form

of specialized consciousness, to gather specific kinds of information critical to the soul's journey. And, of equal importance,
the soul needs the body's legs—the body's very physicality—to
navigate the planet in order to deliver its gifts. Not only a guide,
the body is also the taxi service. Conversely, the body needs the
soul for guidance and a sense of connection; absent this, it floun-
ders in its own suffering. In that respect, the soul is the body's
guide to both heaven and earth. Those complementary needs
create the opportunity and imperative for a partnership, the potential for which is built into the design of who we are as humans.
Complementarity implies, as it turns out, a fundamental quality
of coherence, which is grounded in reciprocity. The Q'ero of
southern Peru (the nation of Don Umberto Sonnco Quispe, whom
I quoted above) teach the fundamental importance of reciprocity,
or *ayni*. All connection demands reciprocity and offers an equal
exchange of energy, information, and support. As the Q'ero recognize, ayni is not automatic where humans are concerned. You
have to choose to do it. In my own way of speaking about it, reciprocity is actualized by coherent connection, which requires both
a choice and skill.

This experiential (before and beyond conceptual) identification with soul consciousness as it looks at the three-dimensional
world through the borrowed senses of the body is what I call a
*soul perspective.* It is simple to say, but more difficult to experience in its raw and primal state.

The nature of soul consciousness evolves from the soul's
initial forgetfulness of who or what it is into a state of focused
attention and soul-self-awareness that allows the soul to take the
lead in forming the partnership with the body. *The Soul's Critical
Path* detailed that evolution. In short, it works like this. Before
the soul comes to the planet to join with a body, it knows itself to
be a soul. Before it arrives upon the planet, it ordinarily forgets
that it is a soul, merging unconsciously into a forming body that
does not yet have the full range of senses that ultimately bring
the soul to its own full self-awareness. Even if it remembers that
it is a soul—as young children often do—culture pretty quickly

discourages that understanding. Immersed unconsciously in the body, something of the soul's nature influences the development of the body and the personality over time through the dynamic of coherence operating at an unconscious level. But that unconscious level of operation does not get us to the level of skill necessary to discover soul purpose.

Through the pain that a body inevitably experiences in life (the fate of all humans), the soul is invited to awaken to itself and rediscover its identity distinct from the body. If it distinguishes itself from the body and shifts identity from body to itself, it has the opportunity to find its origin in the oneness of which it is a distillation. Doing so, it discovers that it can become the conduit of Love—because Love is the nature of the oneness. The soul finds that bringing Love to the body brings the body to an experience of connection and relative safety. Safety is the condition for releasing the trauma that has given rise to the pain in the body. So pain has a purpose—awakening a slumbering soul to its own nature. As the soul leads in healing the body's trauma by sharing the soul's special capacity for constellating Love in the body, the soul can invite the body into a partnership with the soul. That partnership provides legs for the grounding of the soul's purpose on the planet, as well as the means for discovering through the senses of the body what that purpose is.

When the body responds to this soul attention, the body falls in love with the soul, allowing a sense of purpose to emerge in the body in a far more conscious way than in the faint bubbling of intuition that tickles our ordinary body-based consciousness. An unconscious soul provides a trickle of intuition. A conscious, self-identified soul in a relatively healed body provides a pipeline of intuition. This evolutionary sequence has the odor of cosmic design. That design leads to an open-ended process in which the awakened and purposeful soul can collaborate in the creation that offers all souls their destiny. Fate is inevitable. It consists of the challenges inherent to all of our lives. Destiny is not inevitable. It consists of the skillful action of an awakened soul in relation to a changing planet. What brings us from our fate to our destiny is the cultivation of a soul skill that uses the body's sensuality to reach into the ever-changing stream of the world to find what resonates with the soul's inherent gift, day by day.

## The Soul as Field

Speaking of the soul metaphorically as a singular vibration evokes a broader metaphor. A vibration, in scientific parlance, is an electromagnetic field. When one field encounters another field, they communicate and affect each other. They are said, in the language of quantum physics, to *entangle*. If they do so in a harmonic way, they are said to be in *resonance*. When they can't harmonize, they are in a state of *dissonance*. Either way, the fields are connected. They exchange energy and information. If they are each harmonic within themselves, then each is *coherent,* and their communication reflects that coherence.

While there is an inherent resonance, or connection, between soul and body, that resonance may not be sufficiently tuned for the information flow to work well. To work well, or harmonically, is what is implied by the notion of coherence. With an incoherent connection, it is as though there is static in the connection. Tuning that connection to one of harmony is the job of developing soul skills, since the human requires some skill to achieve coherence even though coherence is inherent in nature. Despite being part of nature, humans can render themselves incoherent by separating from nature.

I will elaborate upon coherence as I proceed, but I want to mention one important aspect of it here in connection with the soul. Quantum biophysics is beginning to recognize that coherence allows maximum connection while facilitating maximum individuality. Mae-Wan Ho's work illustrates this concept. She describes coherence operating in the world as a kind of quantum jazz, in which an individual can play creatively and harmoniously with the whole while remaining creatively individual. In my soul metaphor, I would say that the soul is the element that represents individual freedom of attention, intention, and imagination, while bringing a unique gift as its contribution to a coherent orchestra. The soul is a singular player in that orchestra. The body is its instrument—what gives voice and volume to the soul. Heaven, earth, and all their inhabitants have the capacity to connect coherently to make up this jazzy orchestra.

## The Now of the Soul

When Asian meditation traditions and their modern Western translations speak of presence and the "now," I would suggest that they are speaking of the *soul's* now. This now is a perspective that resides outside of time and outside of the experience of which the body's senses are so acutely aware. It is the failure to distinguish between the dual entities of soul and body that results in the confusion that a body-identified personality has with the notion of experiencing timelessness from the perspective of the body's senses. To the extent that those traditions do not acknowledge the existence of a relevant and active soul potential, then the timeless now becomes ambiguous in its relationship to the body. Without the soul perspective, it is literally necessary to "leave" the body—to have an out-of-body experience—in order to experience timelessness from a soul perspective not hindered by the body's senses. When we have left the body's sense of separateness and taste the oneness that is the object of so many meditation traditions, we taste that timeless now. With a soul perspective, we can identify that timelessness with who we are, rather than as simply a non-body experience. Then the soul can share that sense of timelessness with the body in the form of Love.

The body has its own now, but that now is quite different from the soul's now. Let's look at the body next.

# 2

# BODY: CONSCIOUSNESS SENSUALIZED

WE MAY BE TEMPTED to think that the body is easier to understand than the soul for the simple reason that the body is so—well—visible and prominent. My sense is that the body is more complex than the soul and no less mysterious. Despite prodigious scientific and medical efforts, I think that our understanding of the body is relatively small. If it were otherwise, we would be doing better than turning pharmaceutical companies loose on children suffering primarily from disconnection. Science is hamstrung because it has no practical means of understanding consciousness and seems prone to the limiting materialist assumption that both consciousness and intelligence arise from the brain. So I need to depart from science here.

The soul represents the *ability* to sense. With its remarkable variety of specialized senses, the body provides to the soul the *means* of sensing. The body is the sensual instrument of the soul. Said otherwise, the body is consciousness sensualized.

A sense is an aspect of intelligence. Every sense gathers and processes information. Gathering and processing information is what intelligence does. The body is a sensual being that gathers and processes information.

We can speak of the entire body as a creature of *sensuality* and include our brains, hearts, guts, emotions, connective tissue, bones, DNA, and all of the commonly recognized senses within that singular category. Yes, DNA is an information-gathering device, working in collaboration with perhaps as many as 100,000 sensors on the edge of individual cell bodies. And every sense is directed toward gathering information that can be used by the soul and body to navigate and create. While the entire body is an information-gathering device, it is an instrument of a more fundamental intelligence that we call consciousness. In other words, body senses experience (knowing), sees it as a whole (visioning), and analyzes it by sensory category into categories of meaning (thinking). Soul is the witness, driver, and ultimate consumer of this elaborate process.

What are the body's individual forms of sense?

## The Commonly Identified Senses

We are all familiar with "the five" senses. We also speak of a sixth sense often called "intuition." In addition to those six, research has identified other senses.

For example, there is the *ovulation sense* (men can sense when women are ovulating, which men may experience as attraction); *thermoception* (the ability to sense whether something is hot or cold without touching it); *lying perception* (the ability to sense whether a smile is genuine or fake and whether the person is lying); *sense of danger during ovulation;* the *sense of danger* in general (gut feeling, hair raising); *equilibrioception* (the sense of balance); *proprioception* (the ability to sense location of a body part without looking at it); *magnetoception* (the ability to sense direction); sense of time (duration and specific time); and the ability to distinguish facial muscles that indicate happiness, on the one hand, and depression, on the other.

Certainly, this is an incomplete list. My point here is simply to identify such sensory functions as part of the body, rather than the soul. In Part Two I will suggest a functional way of grouping these senses into three broader categories of intelligence that have a natural collaborative relationship with one another, at least when we learn to coordinate them from a soul perspective. In a general way of speaking, soul is the source of intelligence in the human trilogy. Body is the mechanism of intelligence. Heart is how soul, body, and the world work together, through the dynamic of coherence, to put intelligence to work in service of soul purpose.

Before I get to that perspective, let me suggest another away of talking about body intelligences as a sensual function.

## Analytic Understandings: Sensing Meaning

One process our intelligence uses to derive information and meaning is to break things down into parts, which I'll call the analytic function. The analytic function uses categories long identified to manipulate information, such as logic, critical thinking, numbering, rationality, and reasoning. This type of intelligence creates understandings.

I will elaborate upon analytic intelligence under the heading of *thinking* in Part Two, as one part of the trilogy of body-based intelligences upon which the general intelligence of the soul is dependent. My point here is to identify this analytic form of intelligence as a sense. It is the means by which we sense meaning.

## Vision: Sensing Relation

While analysis breaks our experience into parts, we have a complementary sense that puts all of the parts back together into a big picture. There are various categories of intelligence that we can identify with this larger sense: imagery, musical patterning, pattern recognition in general, facial recognition, systems, and so on. This global sense has to do with what I will label *vision*.

While the early work by Roger Sperry resulted in a popularization of dividing the brain into hemispheric halves for such functions as analysis and vision, brain science is more open now to a whole brain capacity for piecing these functions together. Nevertheless, both of these functions certainly seem to arise around the head, while the more recent identification of the heart as a source of intelligence seems to point to a phenomenon that resides in the chest. Science has given little attention to the chest as a source of intelligence.

Again, as with the analytic function of human intelligence, I will elaborate in Part Two upon vision as a second part of the trilogy of body-based intelligence upon which the general intelligence of the soul is dependent. In general, this visionary capacity is also a sense. It is the means by which we sense how things fit together. It is how we sense relation in terms of connecting the individual dots that are recognized by our analytic function.

## Emotions: Sensing Feelings

Emotions express in the body. We are familiar with how emotion is often our first reaction to a change in the environment. Because we move so quickly from the raw experience of change to the body's emotional reaction to the change, the common human experience of emotions is about reaction. So we more often talk about emotions in their reactive state.

However, if the soul is well connected to the body and the body is relatively calmed by the presence of the soul, the soul uses the body's emotional sense as a way to gather raw experience that comes to the body externally. If the soul's presence calms the body sufficiently, the soul may examine the incoming information without the interference of reaction, instead using the emotional sense as a lens. For example, when you encounter someone who is suffering sadness, you may feel the sadness in your own emotional field. With the ability to distinguish your own emotional state and reactions from those of another person, your emotional sense allows you to gather the information that the other person is indeed sad. The arrival of that emotional information is raw experience. So, with emotions we can sense feelings.

## Gut: Sensing Danger

The body has the ability to sense the presence of danger. That raw sense is not fear. Just as our emotional sense may quickly move from informational intake to reaction, the raw sense that danger is present may give way instantly to a fear reaction. However, if the soul is well connected to the body and the body is relatively calmed by the presence of the soul, then the sensed presence of danger is mere information to the soul even as the body may lean in the direction of readiness to meet the source of danger.

For the purposes of the process I describe in this book, it is not important whether our inherent ability to sense danger is specific to the gut or is part of the general knowing sense that I will assign to the heart or is simply one more aspect of the emotional sense. We feel different kinds of information in different parts of the body. We feel in our guts, in our chests, in our bones, our connective tissue, and almost everywhere else in the body, in one way or another. The sorting of these feelings, however they arise, is left to the function that I will call "heart," which I will mention briefly below and discuss in more detail in Part Two as the third part of the trilogy of intelligences.

## Intuition: The Subtle Sense

The sense that we often call intuition is also called the sixth sense and by other names as well. These other names could include all the clair-senses: clairvoyance, clairsentience, clairaudience, and so on. As "clair" implies, this sense is where true clarity arises, a clarity from which deeper understandings and broader visions emerge in ways not apparently available to the other common senses. This clair-sense is centrally important to the ability of the soul to connect with the body and navigate the world through the body. And it is perhaps the least understood. Without it, it is impossible for the soul to discover the purpose to which the soul brings its gift.

But—and this is a big but—our usual experience of the intuitional sense is like our usual experience of the emotional sense. It is far more common, with emotion, that we sense the *reaction* we are having to information coming into our sensory fields rather than sensing the information directly without reaction. By the time we sense the incoming information, a thought or emotion has already formed in reaction to the information. In the same way, intuition may move directly to reaction. But before it fuels a reaction, intuition simply provides raw experience. While I will address intuition as a function of heart intelligence in Part Two, my point here is that intuition arises in the body as a function of the body's sensuality.

## Other Aspects of the Body

There are four other aspects of the body that are not senses but reflect qualities of the body that define the body's operation in relationship to soul and heart. These include the nature of the body as a liquid crystalline organism, the personality, desire, and the body's "now."

## Body as a Liquid Crystalline Structure

In her book *The Rainbow and the Worm: The Physics of Organisms,* British biologist Mae-Wan Ho suggests that her research shows the body, like all organisms, to be "completely liquid crystalline."[2] This particular quality provides the body with the capacity to transmit and receive information across its own fields and from outside its fields instantaneously by means of energy exchange operating through the principle of resonance, allowing long-range coordination of body function.[3]

Ho argues that "it is the coherent flow of electricity at all levels that is responsible for organizing living processes."[4] "At all levels" includes the natural electromagnetic rhythms of the earth, the sun, and the moon.[5] Because the entire body responds through resonance to electromagnetic signals, it is susceptible to coordination through a "global orienting field," which is akin to a conductor leading the orchestral body in the symphonic expression it represents.[6] As Ho points out, the heart has the capacity, by virtue of its dominant electromagnetic force in the body, to be such a conductor—when it can achieve *coherence.*

One remarkable implication of Ho's work is that the speed of communication in the body by means of resonant coherence occurs far more broadly and faster than the nervous system of the body can manage on its own. Because communication among body systems can occur instantaneously, it is possible for the body functions to synchronize with each other, led by a central organizing function in the heart when the heart is in a state of coherence.

In short, the body responds to the heart, and the heart responds to attention. Attention, as we will see, is not neutral but is the means by which love is brought to the body as one of its global, orienting fields—the one that is controlled by the soul. It is in this way we begin to see the simplicity of a central message of this book: focus the soul, bring it to the heart, and flood the body with love. Everything else follows from this simple sequence.

More about coherence in Chapter Three.

## *Personality*

What we think of as "personality" also resides in the field of the body, at least until the soul claims its own identity and activates itself as an entity distinct from the body. This personality that has become the focus of Western psychology is perhaps the most visible aspect of our being. It is a large part of "who" we regard a person to be, but it is the least substantial aspect of who we are. It is helpful to think of it as a hologram, or perhaps as similar to a newspaper.

A hologram is a projected image that appears as a three-dimensional form visible to the unaided eye. The image is created by a focused light source projected through a pattern or image, including a photographic negative. The projection creates an apparent reality that is neither real nor illusory, just as an image in a mirror is not an illusion, but a reflection. To change a projection upon a mirror, we do not address the mirror. Instead, one must change what is being reflected. We change an item of clothing and turn on the overhead light to see better. To change the personality, we focus the soul and change how the body relates to the soul.

A newspaper contains the stories of the day. If today is like all of our yesterdays, the newspaper has nothing to report but the same old stories. Similar to the hologram, there is no substance to the stories themselves. They are a reflection of something else that is happening outside of the paper itself. If the stories are going to change, we have to address the action where change occurs, the place from which new stories emerge. Then we can make new news, instead of stack up the old olds.

The question becomes, where is the pattern or story from which the personality is projected day after day? Does it come from the body, or does it come from the soul? The answer is that it comes from both. But if the soul is not active and online, then the personality will reflect only the body's story, which quickly gets to be old news, since it has no capability of changing its dilemma without the soul's focused presence. When we shift our identification to the soul, the soul's active presence in the body gradually changes the experience of the body, and the projected personality reflects the change. An active soul does not "take over" either the body or the personality, but relates to the body in such a way that the body's experience of the environment changes for the better, which in turn changes its projected personality. In that way the personality reflects the presence and influence of the soul.

Working with the personality alone, by addressing how people think about themselves, can provide some change of perspective. In other words, talk therapy can change the way the body/mind looks at itself. But there is a limit to the value of that change. When the body's experience of the world does not include the active presence of the soul, its experience will inevitably reflect a sense of isolation and vulnerability. Without the active influence of an awakened soul, the personality will reflect the perspective of either the helpless, wounded victim or the brave, stoic, but lonely warrior who cannot surrender. Without attending to the soul, psychology is rather limited to rearranging the furniture on the deck. This was a central message of the late radical Jungian James Hillman, who was critical of modern psychology for its abandonment of *psyche.*

# Desire

I try never to believe what I think, but I'm very respectful of it. What I think about desire is speculation reaching for under-standing, a kind of explorational lyric about the deepest of mysteries that remains always elusive to our understandings.

As I piece all of this together, I think that desire fits so well as to have been designed. Desire seems to be the motive force behind all human senses, that which brings the senses to the service of the soul.

The body is driven by desire. There is none among us who does not live in continual desire. Desire is the collective of the senses reaching out to find connection, fueled by whatever degree of life force is available in light of the degree of trauma carried by the body. When that trauma is effectively released and the body is fully open, life force rushes into the body in the abundance provided by the earth's cornucopic energy body.

Desire is the body's inherent response to a state of constant disconnection reaching out for connection that remains ever just out of its grasp. And the closer the body comes to the experience of connection, the greater the desire. The passion of a soul burning with purpose is the edge of the wave of desire unrequited but tasting its furtive objective just a finger's length away, just close enough for spark to arc and pull the finger forward toward an ever-retreating hand that promises what the skillful soul can deliver in an ever-continuing succession of moments. To bring the body along on this ride, the skillful soul will, with every breath of the body, flood the body with the love of heaven and earth and hold the body in a constant state of tolerable disconnection and anticipatory desire, a cresting wave of vulnerability reaching for safety, a desire not satiated that provides constant motive force.

The soul lives in a state of constant connection. Its nature is connection. By contrast, the body lives in a state of constant disconnection, at least relative to the degree of connection experienced by the soul. The body's umbilical cord has been cut from its mother and the Mother at the moment of birth, the one wound that cannot be remedied—the wound that can only be salved, and then only by the soul. When the fully focused soul turns its attention to the body and floods it with love, the body feels the flow of connection but without the possibility of satiation. The soul feeds the never-ending hunger of the body and, doing so, turns the body to the soul's agenda. It is the arcing of romantic love, in which the fantasized partner willingly becomes the object of an insatiable desire. So designed, the body becomes the willing partner of a soul that needs its body for the soul's purpose to unfold in the world. It is the soul that becomes the mother, the Mother, the father, and the Father to the body. And the wild animal of the body in love offers its power to the only one who can ride it, which is the soul to which it is connected.

Absent the flow of love that issues from a focused and self-identified soul, the body experiences the deepest agony that separation represents in the presence of a constant and driving desire for connection. The mere possibility of satiating desire keeps the body in constant motion, and the presence of a soul that offers the nearest facsimile without a complete satiation keeps the body in constant orientation to the soul, and thereby to the soul's agenda.

To live in identification with such a body is life's greatest torture. To live in identification with a soul consciously partnered with a wild and willing body is to ride the most exciting crest of the planetary life force possible. How can we not brave the opportunity to find that sharpened point of attention that scribes the plane of planetary possibility?

Depression is the suppression of that desire and the giving up of the search for it. We experience depression as illness, and it arises from the chronic disconnection that giving up the search for connection represents. By making the soul the active agent in providing the body its sense of connection, we find the primary cure for depression. This is not a cure for the sense of struggle, but a re-tooling of our ability to face struggle with the enhanced life force that connection provides. This re-tooling is the means by which we embrace the archetype of the *luminous warrior—* which is quite different than the fear-based, exploitive warrior that is now the archetype of the American warrior.

Do not diminish your desire or shame it or cover it over with harsh judgments. Do find yourself in the soul and lead that desire into service of your own gifts, so that the gift that you are may find its way to the world. All such gifts are gifts of service, but not all kinds of service represent *your* gift. Find *that* gift. Make its delivery your purpose. You came for *that* mysterious reason.

## Life Force

We all have a sense of the life force that runs through the body. It is perhaps more apparent by its relative absence, as we notice when we are sick, "run down," tired, or feel the process of aging sapping our vitality. Life force is vitality. It comes into the body gently as conception occurs and soul flips on the light of life force. Soul is not its source. As soul enters the room of the body, it flips a switch that allows life force to flow, just as electricity creates the light controlled by the wall switch that you merely flip.

Life force arises from the earth. It rises into the body, not the soul. Again, as with electricity, the soul does not touch it directly, but through the body, just as electricity becomes available to us through a light bulb, the stove, or some other appliance. The body "applies" the life force in a way that serves the soul. And its availability and intensity depend upon the body's ability to convey it. If there is impedance in the body, then the life force cannot flow in its fullness. Impedance is experienced by the various limitations of the body: unresolved trauma, physical injury, poor health, the repression that we experience as depression, and so on. For the soul to access life force and bring it into service of the soul's agenda, the soul must tend the body and facilitate its healing. Healing is about getting access to life force and putting the body—our all-purpose appliance—to work.

The plant medicines taught me about life force. The plant medicines have the ability to open the body and address its impedance by bringing powerful tools to bear in support of the body's healing. While this healing is experienced most intensely in the moment of ceremony, that moment opens the body not only to the soul, but to life force. Soul and medicine hold the body in an intense moment of safety that shifts the limiting effect of trauma, and life force flows in. This accounts for much of the intensity experienced in the plant medicine ceremony.

The message here, in brief, is that life force comes to the body, not the soul, even though the soul switches the body on when it comes and turns off the lights when it leaves.

## The Body's Now

The soul resides in and manifests a timeless *now*—one that manifests as a sense of non-judgmental presence about which whole libraries have been written. That is not the *now* of the body.

The body has its own now. That now is a timeline consisting of all the experiences of the body. Every present experience of the body is added to every other experience of the body in an ever-growing accumulation of experiences that form the history of the body.

In every moment of the body, its entire history is not only present, but indelibly and forcefully present. Every new experience happens in the context of every prior experience. The body's now is a complete and full memory of its history, available to be read by the soul when the body permits the soul to enter fully in. For many of us, much of that history is closeted. Much of that history is a secret we keep not only from others, but from ourselves. Ordinary mental consciousness does not reach into the body's memories of experiences that have proved too difficult to hold in the ordinary consciousness that we call upon to get us through our day to day.

The distinction is not mere intellectual parsing. The distinction is important as a counterpoint to the struggle of meditation traditions in their ongoing effort to teach presence and experience the timeless now in the midst of the body's constant sensory experiences. The distinction is critically important to our understanding of healing itself. There is a role for the timeless now's ability to be present to the timeline of the body, but it is, I will argue, quite different than the ability of the timeless now to take us away from the body's ongoing experience of all its history. We can dissociate the timeless now and our attention from the body, but we may wind up, if that's all we do, more dissociated than when we started. Or we can discover in our soul nature the access to a timeless now that can be re-associated with the body's vast timeline of experience, which is where the deep healing occurs. Soul's now and body's now not only can co-exist, but need to co-exist as the means to heal the body of the effects of its traumatic history and to discover the soul's purpose. In Part Four, I'll describe how that works.

The question of how that occurs in the frame of the body, as distinct from outside it, brings us to the role of the heart.

# 3

# HEART: CONSCIOUSNESS CONNECTED

IN ORDER FOR ME to explain what I mean by *heart*, I need a more precise language than our common definitions offer. I find that language in a healthy and growing body of scientific research that uses the electromagnetic concept of *coherence* to talk about a state of heart that is not inherent, but achievable. So I will start with a brief reference to those scientific resources. Nevertheless, I want to say that I encountered the *experience* of the coherent heart of which I am speaking first, well before I developed an understanding of the experience that had unfolded in my chest and consciousness. My early languaging of the experience spoke only of heart in a general way. When I spoke of the heart in that general way, I wound up qualifying my use to say that I wasn't speaking of the physical heart, the emotional heart, or the heart chakra. What my usage had in common with all of the other usages is that all point to something that happens in the chest. In time, these scientific sources resonated with my experience and ultimately provided another way to talk about heart.

I might have tried to give this coherence function a name other than heart. But I think it would be disingenuous to make up an entirely new term, since this separate function of heart lies subtly beneath all of these other familiar functions. It also lies, experientially, in the same part of the body. Indeed, it may lie directly in the physical heart but be accessible only with skill. And the poets of the ages have used heart as the identifier for the source of the experiences, among others, of which I speak.

There are three sources I would mention as fruitful for your further exploration of heart coherence. These can be found in various publications of the HeartMath Institute, the work of Joseph Chilton Pearce, and the work of biologist Mae-Wan Ho. Both Pearce and Ho have incorporated HeartMath's research into their respective analyses. My borrowing from these resources will be brief and consequently oversimplified. These sources neither justify nor prove my position that the heart is a portal by which the soul operates in connection with the body. None of them say that. I simply mean to suggest that there is research that parallels my metaphor in a supportive way.

## The HeartMath Institute

The HeartMath Institute points out a little-observed fact.[7] The electric field of the heart, measured by a common electrocardiogram (ECG), is about 60 times greater in amplitude than the electric field of the brain. The magnetic field of the heart is about 5,000 times stronger than that of the brain. The ordinary ECG readout represents the typical electrical behavior of the heart, as a measure of heart rate variability, that resembles as much as anything else the jagged profile of a stock market report. HeartMath has shown that this pattern, while typical, is not coherent, but can be rendered so by our intentionally holding attention in the area of the physical heart, breathing in a particularly steady and deep way, and holding the experience of appreciation in the heart. When this happens, the heart is said to have become *coherent.* The coherent heart acts as a master rhythm in the body to which all other body rhythms are entrained despite operating at different frequencies. By various means, including hormone production, sound, pressure waves, and electromagnetic rhythm, the coherent heart becomes the conductor of the rhythmic orchestra of the body.

Even the brain responds to the heart's lead with a shift in its predominant frequencies. With heart coherence, the brain's waves shift toward *alpha* frequency—associated with relaxation of the body. Elsewhere in the body, stress hormones decrease, along with blood pressure. Mood elevates. Even at high levels of physical activity that increase the heart's pulse rate, such symptoms of coherence can take place. With coherence, there is a two-way communication between the heart and the rest of the body that maximizes positive coordination of all body functions.

## Mae-Wan Ho

Mae-Wan Ho agrees with the HeartMath Institute. She says, "The heart certainly provides the most obvious large-scale electromagnetic field that can coordinate the electrical activities of the entire body."[8] But she goes much further. Her research lays the groundwork for transcending the dominant scientific view that the brain is the primary source of coordination for the body's intelligence. Instead, she suggests that the body's intelligence is a function of the body's nature as a single coherent "'photon field' bound to living matter. . . coherent simultaneously in a whole range of frequencies that are nevertheless coupled together. . . . That means energy input to any frequency will become readily delocalized over all the frequencies."[9]

In other words, regardless of what the body senses by means of any particular sensory capacity, the information received will be communicated instantly throughout the entire body and to fields outside the body that are "entangled" with the body's fields. This, Ho says, is the hallmark of biological organization: the quantum delocalization of electromagnetic energy and cooperative interaction.[10] It can occur because the body is made almost entirely of *liquid crystals,* including lipids, DNA, and possibly all proteins, including those in muscles and connective tissue. The body thereby becomes a "tunable responsive system."[11] By virtue of this mechanism, it is possible for an organizing morphogenetic field to direct or influence the development of the embryo from generalized cells to a complex organism with highly specialized cells.[12]

Consciousness, Ho concludes, "is delocalized throughout the liquid crystalline continuum of the body (including the brain), rather than being just localized to our brain, or to our heart." By "consciousness," Ho means "at the minimum, the faculties of sentience (responsiveness), intercommunication, as well as memory."[13] All of this works "much faster than conduction or electrical signals by the nerves. Thus the 'ground substance' of the entire body has a much better intercommunication system than can be provided by the nervous system alone."[14]

Brain consciousness is only a part of this system. Because the brain and body consciousness may "decouple," the "unity of our conscious experience depends on the complete coherence of brain and body." That unity "arises from and depends on quantum coherence."[15] Coherence permits instantaneous communication because there is no separation in time and space, which is another way of saying that a quantum coherent system is made of frequencies "entangled" in the way quantum physics began to speak of non-local action eighty years ago.[16]

What is unique in Ho's work is her application of these notions of quantum physics to biological organisms in a way that corresponds with our own intuition that the soul and the heart deeply influence the operation of the body. As I hold Ho's work next to the metaphor of soul and heart I am using, I find it directly descriptive of how a soul works with a traumatized body in a chaotic world. Ho says, "The key to surviving entangled, it seems, is to remain coherent by bouncing off other coherent systems."[17]

The soul becomes a coherent field in its own right by the steps I will describe in Part Four. Using the heart, the coherent soul can bring the body to a state of coherence that allows the soul to use the sensuality of the body to navigate the world of external fields in order to discover and become entangled with the coherent fields that represent the soul's opportunities to deliver the soul's gifts in meaningful work on the planet. Ho says:

> It involves a consciousness delocalized and entangled with all of nature, when the awareness of self is heightened precisely because self and other are simultaneously accessed. I believe that is the essence of aesthetic or mystical experience.
>
> This manner of knowing—with one's entire being, rather than just the isolated intellect—is foreign to the scientific tradition of the west. . . . We have come full circle to validating the participatory perspective that is universal to traditional indigenous knowledge systems the world over.[18]

## Joseph Chilton Pearce

As is the case with the work of the HeartMath Institute and Mae-Wan Ho, any attempt to represent Joseph Chilton Pearce's work in a paragraph or two feels disrespectfully inadequate. Again, my purpose is simply to point a scientifically interested reader in that direction and to borrow some further concepts about coherence.

Pearce has also acknowledged HeartMath's work and written about it extensively. His work deals with the evolution of human consciousness, with particular attention to the process of development of the prefrontal cortex, which he calls the "fourth brain." Pearce's consistent message is that a coherent heart is central at all stages of development to the formation of the brain structures upon which human potential depends. Without mother's love, modeled upon the love that a mother earth has long provided humanity, a child's physiology cannot mature into an adult physiology capable of love, kindness, and creativity. Pearce writes:

If the mother herself is given a safe, protective environment, free of anxiety and threat (or, if she can create and maintain such a state within herself, as humans can), her infant will be born with an enlarged fore-brain and a reduced hind-brain. If the expectant mother feels in a harsh, unsafe anxiety-ridden, or threatening environment, her infant will be born with a reduced fore-brain, larger hind-brain, and a larger skeletal structure and muscular mass.[19]

Pearce certainly sees human evolution occurring, if at all, as a result of a resonant interaction between the fields of an individual human and the external fields that guide human development; and he says that the purpose of this guidance is creativity on the planet, not escape from planetary suffering:

Field-effects, be they cosmological or ideological, can become active structures of knowledge and function as readily as any part of a mind-set, such as our sensory system's response to environment. To live in Spirit and truth is to translate grace through one's action in gravity.[20]

. . . Again, a resonant dialogue between body and Spirit, grace and gravity, is called for. The trick is to know when to work, and when to do nothing except open.[21]

## The Heart Portal

The heart of which I speak is not a place, but a *process* that arises when certain conditions arise within the region of the physical heart. The process requires intention, imagination, attention, and skill. I think it is this process these scientific efforts are identifying with the notion of coherence.

We are certainly aware that the brain can express either intelligently or unintelligently. In the same way, the physical heart can express intelligently or unintelligently. Because it is uncommon to think of the heart as a source of intelligence, we might more likely say that the physical heart can express in greater or lesser degrees of health. But I want to speak of the function of the heart portal as an expression of intelligence.

Regarding the heart, we can observe intelligent operation when certain conditions are present. If we think of the soul as the conscious *observer*—not a neutral observer, but an observer with an ultimate agenda of creativity—then we can think of the body as the soul's ultimate *instrument* of observation. But bodies and souls commonly inhabit the same space without giving rise to much intelligence. There is a third something that links even a conscious, self-identified soul to the full instrumentation that is the body's array of sensualities. That third something is the condition of *coherence* in the region of the physical heart. Certainly, we know the heart can operate for a lifetime without ever achieving coherence. But when the heart moves into a state of coherence, a focused, self-identified soul can peer into the body's fully developed sensuality (when not limited by the blocking effect of unconsciously held trauma) and read both the body and the world through the body. That state of heart coherence, in combination with the developed soul and fully available sensuality of the body, is the portal that I am also calling *heart*. What the soul experiences by way of a coherent heart operating in a clear body I call *knowing*. So the aspect of potential human intelligence associated with the heart is "knowing." When that knowing moves out to the brain, it can foster critical thinking or visioning, or both.

While the heart of which I speak is a process, it is a process humans must create from skillful means. The physical heart is created for us. The emotional heart is a metaphor that we have created because of the natural associations made between the emotional sensations felt in the chest and the physical heart also located there; and that emotional heart is similarly created for us. The heart *chakra* is, relative to the physical heart, a more subtle field, but it is a standing field also created for us. Only the heart portal requires an intentional, imaginal, attentional skill to create. All three of these "created" hearts may operate either functionally or dysfunctionally. When we are able to work the heart portal, soul, and body in skillful collaboration, then the physical heart, emotional heart, and heart chakra are drawn into a harmonic resonance that brings each into optimal efficacy. That is the direct experience I have observed while working with clients on my massage table.

When the coherent soul entrains the physical heart, then the portal heart is created. By creating heart coherence, the soul tunes the body in the direction of its own coherence. The soul invites the body to come to an internal harmony. It does this with resonance. It does so through the body's heart for a simple reason. More than any other aspect of the body, the heart has the ability, by virtue of its dominant electromagnetic field and the phenomenon of resonance, to bring all of the other frequencies of the body into coherence—the state of harmonic operation that Mae-Wan Ho has called *quantum jazz*. She sees these diverse musicians working in distinctly different rhythms and notes that somehow represent a harmony. Working differently within the same key and rhythm is much like coherence. Because the physical heart provides the strongest field in the body, it can entrain a weaker field. If it is coherent, it can foster coherence in the rest of the body.

So, the heart of which I speak here is a function of neither body nor soul, unless one sees it as a potential or unactivated capacity of the physical heart. Either way, it exists as an intersection between body and soul, as the means by which the infinite soul can connect with a finite body and by which the sensuality of the body and the consciousness of the soul can experience their inherent connection with everything else.

Heart is both the third part of the human trinity and the third part of the trilogy of human intelligences. As a form of intelligence, I will take heart up again in Part Two. Here, I want merely to identify heart as a phenomenon, function, and process unto itself, and I want to be clear that I am talking about something that is different than what is commonly referred to by the same name.

*** 

In this way, a human is a mysterious trinity—a union consisting of three distinct processes that have the potential of collaboration: soul, body, and heart portal. Each of these three has a distinct form of intelligence that manifests only when we develop the skill to bring each to a state of coherence. When each is coherent, the three can collaborate to manifest the greater potential of human intelligence. The potential of bringing those three forms of intelligences into a skillful collaboration is the subject of Part Two. The process for doing so is the subject of Part Four.

PART TWO

# HOW IT WORKS: THE TRILOGY OF HUMAN INTELLIGENCE

# INTRODUCTION TO
# PART TWO

THE PHENOMENON OF INTELLIGENCE, human or otherwise, remains a mystery.

Conventional science assumes that intelligence is located in the brain, without sufficient evidence to support what is at best a theory masquerading as dogma. Conventional educational policy assumes that intelligence is located in books and that it can be transplanted into immature brains by a pedagogical process reflected in present-day public school education policy. We are currently experiencing the deep inadequacy of that assumption, while public policy flails at filing children quietly in their desks like data storage media before indenturing a few of them through the college industry to the Wall Street and technology sweepstakes, leaving the rest to fill in the sinking space that was once occupied by the middle class.

That educational thinking actually originated during the period of Enlightenment, which was followed rather quickly by the emergence of the Age of Reason. But the context of educational thinking was different then, certainly intended for less than universal access, as is now the case. It was during that time that philosophers such as John Locke began to reclaim from the Catholic Church the right of the individual to tend one's own soul. The emergent argument was that one could have one's own mind and read the Divine Mind without the intervention of the Church.

The Ages of Reason and Enlightenment opened the door to secular science. However, as science was able to find its feet by separating from the Church, it also ultimately separated from matters of spiritualty and soul. The absence of "scientific" evidence for the existence of the soul came, in the hands of lesser scientific thinkers, to constitute evidence for the absence of the soul, and God as well. This growing domination by a more narrow scientific movement in turn opened the door to a secular psychology also cut off from its roots in the *psyche,* originally synonymous with the idea of soul. Consequently, modern and mainstream science looks only to the intellect—a subset of intelligence that focuses on the capacity for thought—that has zero capacity to sense the presence of soul.

Which leads to an irony worth observing.

The great thinkers of the Age of Reason and the Enlightenment worked very hard to wrest the soul back from religion, so that individuals could tend their own souls and discover a personal morality grounded in a direct connection with God. These pioneers created room for science to emerge and for souls to gain traction in the material world. In the meantime, science has devolved into a materialistic and increasingly opportunistic enterprise that has returned any concern for individual souls to the Church. Giving soul concerns back to the Church has left the prospect of a direct connection between ordinary humans and God without institutional support, a point I will address more directly in Part Three.

With all of this, and despite the technical advances of science, there remains an absence of any consensus on the meaning of intelligence. Since I'm going to talk about intelligence, I need to start with a definition. Again, as was the case with my defining what I mean by "heart," I came to my own understanding about intelligence from my own experience. I have found sources that provide a frame of reference for communicating those ideas without purporting to demystify the source of intelligence itself.

With just a little looking, it was possible to find common cause with Plato and Aristotle, who came to conclusions that seemed to better describe my experience than do current science and psychology. And those perceptions tracked some of the thinking that initiated the Age of Reason, while soul was still a recognized player in the field of intelligence, before science suspended it from the game.

Aristotle distinguished sense perception, imagination, and reason from another quality he called *nous*. Nous, Aristotle explained, is a quality of the soul, and soul (or psyche) is what animates the body. Soul, in Aristotle's view, brings with it the ability to be aware, and awareness—nous—is what *uses* sense perception, imagination, and reason. Soul's nous provides the *ability to understand* to the brain's *ability to reason* in light of the information derived from the body's *ability to sense*. A particular understanding is the product of that process and is subject always to further sense perceptions and further reasoning that may modify the always provisional understanding that preceded the current one.

As I look at Aristotle's categories of intelligence, I find a direct parallel with what I am calling *knowing* (sense perception), *thinking* (reason), and *vision* (imagination). These three capacities are activated and used by the awareness that is the primary quality of the soul.

If we are alive, we have awareness. Any level of awareness will, in turn, allow activation of the ability to think, envision, and sense so long as the physical platforms of those capacities are not impaired. However, without the concentration of awareness that a fully awakened, self-identified, totally focused soul represents, the faculties of thinking, visioning, and sensing remain dim lights at best. Unfortunately, what the Age of Reason accomplished in taking the soul out of the hands of the Church, which the Church had taken from the hands of such skilled souls as Plato and Aristotle, has now been almost completely lost as modern science-lite has returned the care of the soul back to religion.

What struck me about Locke's view of the relationship between the self and the soul is its parallel with the dominant paradigm among modern alternative healing practices, which presume the soul's distance from the body/mind/personality to be a source of malady—a malady that Locke felt could be cured by the body/mind side of the relationship with soul. The cure, in the modern expression of indigenous healing traditions, is to "retrieve" the soul by bringing it back to the body. As the indigenous tradition has been translated to modern culture and aligned with modern psychology, there is a line of thought that the soul is fragile, subject to fragmentation by the experience of trauma in the body. To heal the trauma, the thinking goes, the soul must be tracked to where it has hidden itself from the trauma outside the body and returned to restore peace and health to the body. The soul, this view contends, must be tended with kindness and compassion. This interpretation of indigenous tradition views the body/mind/personality as the natural location of the human identity and the soul as both fragile and loosely connected. The soul, in this traditional view, is retrieved to the personality. All of this seems consistent with Locke's view.

I no longer engage either this view or this practice. My experiences suggest to me just the opposite. It is the soul that is immortal. The body/mind/personality is by far more "fragile" than the soul. The soul, while immortal, can seem fragmented, but more in the way that attention can be fragmented, dispersed, or distracted. As we experience throughout our days, it is easy for our attention to be distracted if we do not have the skill to focus it. Focused attention is perhaps the most rare commodity on the planet. And it is a highly sought-after commodity, as the competition for your attention by modern forms of media now reflects.

The reason that soul and body tend to remain separate is found more in the vulnerability of the body. It is the body that suffers trauma and holds the memory of trauma. In response to trauma, the body experiences pain and forms its own defensive posture. Both the trauma and the defensive strategy are held by the body, while the mind typically remains unconscious of both the defensive dynamic and the underlying trauma. Mind, responsible for our day-to-day functioning, finds ways to deny the historic trauma by leaving it to the unconscious nature of the body's memory. The body's memory of trauma is independent from any conscious mental memory of the trauma. In this unconscious posture, the body suffers the pain and discomfort that arise from the body's sense of isolation. When the soul shines its light of awareness through such a body, the body's sense of its own pain and isolation is initially amplified for the simple reason that the soul's presence increases body awareness. The soul's growing presence can consequently be experienced by the body as an intensification of its pain. The body's reaction can be to push the awareness away by "dissociating" or numbing the pain that is the very indication of the soul's presence. So soul and body do separate, but the separation is the consequence of the body's fragility, not a fragility of the soul. Our lack of skill in holding focus in the soul—attention—contributes to the dissipation of the soul. The soul is either focused or not, but it is not fragile.

So, instead of working with my clients to do "soul retrievals," as the American shamanism industry now teaches, I do "body retrievals." As I will detail in Part Four, the process of shifting identity to the soul and strengthening its power by the skill of focusing awareness into a laser-like attention allows the soul to become the active agent in bringing soul and body together.

It is from this soul perspective that I will talk about the three intelligences of the body and why each is important if we are to discover and activate soul purpose by means of the body's sensuality. Grouping the body's broad range of sensuality into forms of intelligence, we find *knowing (*the experience of connection), *thinking* (the integration of experience), and *visioning* (sensing relationship). Each of these intelligences is a tool for gathering *and* processing information. What uses these sensual tools is the soul.

I'll start with knowing.

# 4

# KNOWING: THE EXPERIENCE OF CONNECTION

## *Fishing*

WHEN I WAS A YOUNG TEEN, a friend and I went fishing in a small mountain stream. I had fished in lakes, but I had never caught a fish in moving water, which I presumed to be entirely different. "How will I know," I asked my more experienced teacher, "if I get a bite?"

Ron, my equally young fishing master, said simply, "You'll know."

As my bait bobbed upon a white ripple in the center of the current, the end of my rod bobbed as well. Was that a bite? "How will I know if I get a bite?" I repeated, feeling a little nervous that I might not respond at the critical moment. Ron stuck with the enigmatic "You'll know." He could have tried to explain what a bite felt like, but he was wise enough not to take the bait my question's hook offered.

Ron suggested that I let out some line so that the bait could float into a pool shaded by a large pine tree. Doing so would take the bait out of sight, where I would have to rely entirely on the feel of the rod. As the bait flowed over a small drop into the pool, my pole bent sharply forward. I knew I had a bite. And I knew that I knew.

There were two knowings here, along with some thinking that resulted in two understandings. My body senses registered the sensation of a fish taking the hook. The fish's pull was translated to my senses as it travelled through the hook, line, and pole in such a way that I could feel the presence and strength of the fish pulling away. I instantly *knew* that I had made a connection. The sensation was unmistakable. The context provided the elements that allowed for interpretation. In addition to the raw experience of the pull on my line and the bend of the pole, we intended and expected to catch a fish. There was a stream. We understood fish lived there. Fish are attracted to food. And so on. In that context, and with the sensation coming through the pole in my hands, a thought arose. The thought was to this effect: "That is a fish on my line." The thought, taking the context into account, processed the sensation and gave meaning to it. At the same time, I was aware not only of the sensation of the fish, but also of the sensation of the thought about the fish. The observer—the soul—was aware of the sensation of a thought that processed the primary knowing. I knew I had a bite, and I knew I had a thought. Two knowings.

And there were two understandings. The first understanding was clearly an interpretation of the sensation on my line, giving rise to the understanding that a fish was on my line. The second understanding was the one that answered the question of how I would know. The answer was "I know. That's how I know."

And in the background of this sequence, my imagination had envisioned the possibility that a fish might be feeding in the dark pool in the shadow of the tree. So the body allowed the soul a view—through a collaboration of vision, knowing, and thinking—of the sense of hooking a fish and an understanding of how it all came together—all in an instant. In that instant, there were several processes working simultaneously and working together.

# Knowing as Raw Experience

Knowing is a reaching into, an awareness moving into, a merger with something that I am not: a fish, the flame of a fire, another person, another dimension of reality. It is a direct engagement with other, including the body itself as other to the distinctly separate soul. And there are two realms, possibly but not necessarily distinct, into which the awareness reaches.

One of these realms is that of matter, where the mortal body lives. The body seems specially designed to sense within this realm, but not necessarily so limited as we imagine. The soul awareness operating through the body's sensuality can connect with everything in this realm through the sensuality of the body.

There is another realm—quite evidently not apparent to everyone's senses—that consists of something other than matter. When we speak of the awareness leaving the body—having an out-of-body experience—the soul enters into or connects with that other or those other realms. When it does, the soul awareness might be on its own, not using the body's senses. Or the soul may have some experience of the other realms with some assistance of the body's extraordinary senses. The answer to that question lies in deconstructing our ability to engage other-dimensional archetypal figures within a light field apparent to the senses of the body, what we call hallucinations even when we mean to describe experiences that are real. My mind is not, nor yours, I suspect, fully capable of making an accurate interpretation of these different experiences in terms of how the soul uses or doesn't use the body's sensuality in this non-material realm. My confusion begs the question whether the non-material realm is actually separate or merely more subtle in relation to the body's ordinary forms of sensuality. Perhaps, when the soul travels "out-of-body," it is using the body's senses in a different way. I don't understand it, but I can certainly experience it.

In *The Soul's Critical Path,* I related a story of a near-death experience that occurred during a deathbed psychodrama exercise that was part of a shamanic training. As I left my body, I recall that the leaving of the body seemed complete, just as I experienced during the ayahuasca ceremony of which I spoke in the Introduction. In both instances, I had no body sensation during the journey, but I was receiving information that seemed to register on the body's sensuality. The notion of quantum entanglement might provide a theory here, if not an understanding.

Leaving my body on the massage table that served as the imagined deathbed, I had no awareness of my body that I can recall. Yet, as I journeyed, I had visions and heard voices. My mind interpreted the ultimate destination of the journey as the soul's home, the place from which the soul had originated. I distinctly recall *feeling* that the "place" was "home." My interpretation of home was from the raw experience of the feeling itself. I felt completely connected. I was aware of, but could not see, the presence of others. I felt that my presence was acknowledged and that I acknowledged the presence in turn. My vision, at the point of that destination, perceived an undifferentiated whiteness of diffuse light.

Certainly, this was raw experience. Certainly, there was sensation. Certainly, my mind was present and actively interpreting the events. Yet when I re-entered the body, the flood of sensation that exploded in my consciousness was, compared to the ecstatic nature of what had gone on during the out-of-body experience, almost overwhelming. Although the sense of connection was palpable and clear, the intensity of sensations that accompanied my return to the body itself seemed multiplied by comparison. Was the out-of-body experience body-sensation based? I can't say. Perhaps the soul has its own senses that become apparent when the soul activates the body. Actual death might provide the raw experience that could answer that question. So my understanding is provisional.

But there is one interpretation that seems crystal clear, to me at least, as I have worked with these dynamics over several years. The soul's *purpose* cannot be discerned without the active, daily engagement between the body's sensuality and the world of matter in all its complexity. Soul purpose is an earth-based journey, and the earth is its partner. I will elaborate upon how this works in Part Four. But, for now, I want to emphasize that raw experience provides a direct knowing apprehended by the soul through the active engagement of the body's sensuality; and that raw experience of the world of non-matter, if there is such a distinction to be made, is far more subtle, is far less full-bore sensual, and says less about purpose in the moment to moment of our lives.

What the out-of-body sense *does* speak to is the question of who we are. From such experiences, my mind cannot escape the conclusion that who I am is not the body, but a consciousness that is attached to this body, one that I choose to call the *soul*.

## The Depth of Raw Experience

The body let my soul awareness encounter the experience of the fish. But the body is not so accommodating overall. Will the body allow itself to be so filled by soul that the body's sensuality is given over to the awareness of more subtle experience, including both the innermost experience of the body itself and the experience of other realms while awareness is still deeply connected to the body?

Can we have the raw experience of the personality of another person as they enter the room? Can we sense movement in the zeitgeist, such as is being revealed by the presidential campaign in the United States as I write these words in 2016? Can we sense the presence of synchronistic opportunities moment by moment as we go through our lives day by day? Can we sense the presence of other-dimensional guides who would whisper in our ears were we to give such opportunity our full attention?

At least some of these experiences require deep levels of body sensuality. For such levels of knowing, the soul must be fully focused and the body must be fully available, beyond the limitations imposed by unconscious defenses built around historic traumas. Defenses must be dropped along with denial of the trauma. The soul must have engaged the heart portal and induced a state of coherence in the heart. And the soul must have brought the body to a level of safety—itself a way of talking about body coherence—that will permit the soul to fully engage the body's sensuality in all of its subtlety. Is the body willing to put down the filters that it has created in the mind to defend the body against the exigencies of the world? Will the body be able to set its fears aside to admit entirely new and raw experience to enter the space of its capacity for sensing both subtle and non-subtle experiences?

These are questions of process, which means we answer them as we explore our own capacity for reaching deeper and deeper experience, and heal what impedes our access to experience. What does that deeper experience feel like? You'll know. For the purpose of my narrative, I need only say that raw knowing is the primary source of information by which we competently navigate the world, including the discovery and engagement of our purpose. It is distinct from and precedes the interpretation that thinking brings to our experience in order to give it meaning. And it is distinct from the visioning of possibilities that may precede or follow any particular experience.

## The Condition of Connecting through Coherence

We gain the raw experience that is the foundation of our knowing only by connecting, as I connected with the fish. How do we connect?

I rise in the morning. I look out the window. I see the sun rising. I *know* the sun is rising. I *think*, "The sun is rising." I *know* my body is sluggish, but awakening. I *think*, "My body feels tired." We tend to bracket our thoughts as though they are the first awareness of what is going on. Yet *knowing*—direct experience apprehended by the sensuality of the body—precedes the bracketing of that experience into thought.

Remember, if you will, the feeling of deeply loving someone, such as the love a parent can feel for a child. Notice where in your body you feel it. Notice that the feeling does not require a thought or an explanation or an understanding. The feeling requires no proof or validation of its existence. While we may acknowledge to ourselves that the feeling has arisen or exists, its presence does not require a mental acknowledgment. We have many feelings that are never acknowledged. The feeling simply exists, and it resides within our body consciousness without any conscious thought of its being necessary. It just is. We know it because we feel it in our chest and perhaps throughout our body. The experience of the love exists without our having to *think* that the love exists.

When I ask people how they know they love their child, they often look puzzled. They just know. They don't have to think about it, and no amount of thinking would prove or disprove the sensation—the knowing—that they love their child. If I ask where they know this love of their child, they often again look puzzled for a moment, then point to their chests.

I watched a YouTube video of Mae-Wan Ho participating in a scientific panel discussion. Answering a question, she ended her response with the comment "I know it in my heart." I thought to myself, here is the only woman on a panel of otherwise male scientists. She has the courage to say what her own research has come to support. And she says it with such authority that the phrase "I know it in my heart" becomes a credible interpretation of careful scientific observation. In this response, she courageously challenges the bulwark of Western science that claims to know, without adequate investigation, that intelligence and knowing are functions of the brain, all the while confusing what I am calling "knowing" with what I am calling "understanding."

Many of you have also said to yourself or another person, "I know it in my heart." That indeed happens, and it happens when the heart has brought some or all of the body senses into the kind of harmony that makes them available to sense what the mind cannot observe directly but must observe at the distance of inference. The mind infers from raw experience.

The heart, on the other hand, knows. What we know in our hearts is what we often call intuition. Intuition comes in small ways and large. It comes frequently when our hearts have tuned the sensuality of the body to connect coherently with the greater world outside the body, so that information ordinarily unavailable becomes suddenly available. Sometimes that intuition arises to give us information about people with whom we are intimately connected. That is easy to understand in terms of unconscious coherence. We are often in resonant connection—coherently connected—with those that we love, not because we are skilled in rendering our hearts coherent, but because that deep connection is *inherently* coherent. The soul has the capacity to constellate the greater capacity of infinite or cosmic Love into our hearts, giving rise to the possibility of becoming *skillfully* coherent with the coherent fields that surround us even more profoundly than occurs with family and friends.

The coherent heart is the way in which the soul and body sense *the resonance of connection* and, through that sense, the higher-amplitude connections that point the soul to the relationships, pathways, and opportunities that shape its potential destiny. While our capacity for analysis and vision stands at a certain distance from the object of our attention, the heart allows us to *move into* the object and experience it directly—*to know it*—even before we can understand it as part of a larger puzzle of our connections. In a manner of speaking, by connecting with the heart, we know an object otherwise separate from the soul and body by *becoming* that object; we know it from its inside as we bring our inside into that other. We turn our attention inside out, and we merge.

Ho speaks of this dynamic quite eloquently:

> The dilemma of the absolutely ignorant external observer betrays the alienation from nature that the mechanistic scientific framework of the west entails, for it is premised on the separation of the observer as disembodied mind from an objective nature observed.

That is also the origin of the subjective-objective dichotomy, which, when pushed to its logical conclusion, comes up against the seemingly insurmountable difficulty that in order to have sufficient information about the system, one has in effect to destroy it.

But. . . one can infer a great deal about the micro-state of the system by *allowing* the system to inform. In other words, we must find ways of *communicating* with the system itself, rather than interrogating it, or worse, testing it to destruction. . . .

Ideally, we should be *one* with the system so that the observer and observed become mutually transparent or coherent. . . . Perhaps such a state of enlightenment is just what Plato envisaged as being one with the Divine Mind; or as the *Taoists* of ancient China would say, being one with the *Tao*, the creative principle that is responsible for all the multiplicity of things. It involves a consciousness delocalized and entangled with all of nature, when the awareness of self is heightened precisely because self and other are simultaneously accessed. I believe that is the essence of aesthetic or mystical experience [italics in original].

This manner of knowing—with one's entire being, rather than just the isolated intellect—is foreign to the scientific tradition of the west. But I have just demonstrated that it is the only authentic way of knowing. . . . We have come full circle to validating the participatory perspective that is universal to traditional indigenous knowledge systems the world over.[22]

Soul provides the perspective and body provides the means for participation with "one's entire being." This is how we know. The soul aims the body's sensuality toward, connects with, and enters into other to know other, something we can then no longer depersonalize or objectify as an "it." All of nature permits this intimacy and resides in this intimacy, except as nature becomes so wounded that it will defend against that invasive entry. We experience that defensiveness in our own bodies when the focused soul first attempts to enter the body still beset with and defended around its traumas. We experience that defensiveness when we offer to connect intimately with animals and other humans whose traumas have set up defensive shields.

Experience arises through every aspect of the body's diverse sensualities. We do not have to understand what those aspects are, how many there are, or even what they do. When we recognize a face, we do not have to stop to think that we have the capacity for facial recognition, or analyze the elements of the face and understand what we have recognized. We do not have to stop and turn that capacity on because we observe a face approaching. All of the body's sensualities are automatic, meaning they are triggered into action by the presence of an inherent *connection* that has become active at the level of inception of *relationship,* created by turning and tuning our attention. Relationship means that we have turned our attention to something to which we are already connected. Skillful relationship begins to arise when we turn the attention of a focused soul residing in the timeless now to something to which we are already connected.

In a very general sense, it is true that everything is connected to everything else. Quantum physics is coming to this conclusion. Esoteric spirituality has long said the same. But the existence of connection is not the same as relationship. Relationship is an increase in the amplitude of a particular connection. If a tree falls in the forest, I hear it only if I am in the forest with the tree, because the proximity of my ordinary capacity for attention in the forest causes my sensuality to have a greater intensity of connection than if I were standing in the city. I am connected to every tree on the planet, but in relationship only with those to which I bring my conscious attention in one way or another. We can bring our capacity to knowing a tree with our ears, but there are so many other ways that our body sensualities can relate to a tree through our inherent connection with trees. But these other kinds of relationships demand other kinds of sensual skills.

The shift from general connection to particular relationship gives rise to deeper, more intimate experience. That experience is apprehended by the body's sensuality because the attention of the soul is intentionally directed toward the amplification of a particular connection, or the object of connection addresses its presence toward our attention. Either I call you, or you call me. The latent connection provided by our inactive sense-phones is activated into relationship when we get online with each other. I can notice the tree, or it can notice me. Noticing, as quantum physics has noticed, is what brings relationship into being. Noticing activates experience, and experience arises in some aspect of the body's sensuality.

With any experience, the direct and immediate result is a *knowing* at the level of the body's sensuality. It is not different in essence from our ability to feel whether the stove is hot or cold. We know through direct experience the presence of heat or cold through our ordinary senses. Our thinking follows the experience so quickly—*Oh my! The stove is hot, and I've burned my finger*—that we might easily think that our experience and thought are simultaneous. But experience indeed preceded the thought.

I realize that the word *knowing* is often used to express the same idea as facts, understandings, information, and even theories. But I am using *knowing* in a way that is limited to direct experience in order to distinguish it from the other forms of intelligence that humans possess. With a hot stove, we might think our experience was in the finger, or in the connective tissue, or in the neurology. That is a question science is welcome to parse. You and I don't need to understand where the experience occurs in order to deduce from the experience the understanding that represents an abstraction of the experience: the stove is hot. The idea that the stove is hot is indeed an idea, a thought, a quantum of information, an understanding that represents an experience reduced to a thought. The thought is not the same as the original experience that gave rise to the thought.

The thought, once in our minds, is a thing in itself. Our awareness can visit the thought. That visit is called *remembering*. When we remember the hot stove through visiting the thought that emerged from the experience of the hot stove, we experience not the hot stove, but the mind's abstraction of the experience of the hot stove. And, as body/mind research has suggested, the visit to that memory may trigger a replay of the experience held at the level of sensual memory, a phenomenon quite different than abstract memory. There are these two kinds of memory. So understandings of experience become the source of new and distinct experience, just as the body's reliving an otherwise unconsciously held memory is a new experience.

The accumulation of these kinds of experience results in ordinary understandings that help us navigate the world. That accumulation is what we have called common sense. Common sense—those understandings that arise directly from our own experiences—comes from knowings.

It is the same with all knowing, although all knowing does not arise in the same way. The body has many forms of sensuality. Some knowings seem more subtle than, for example, the experience of a hot stove. My love for my children is not particularly subtle, but my experience of the presence of my destiny calling me to my purpose to be found in the possible options of this day has seemed subtler and more difficult to experience, until I learned how to experience it more deeply. Only occasionally does the dynamic of destiny act like a hot stove in getting our attention.

We seldom have the experience of a single experience moving toward a thought moving toward an envisioning of possibility. It is far more common to be having multiple experiences all at once while our minds attempt to process them all at once. It is often overwhelming. It is probably why our minds contain filters that limit incoming information as much as minds also function as receivers of information. There is more experience to experience than we can process in a moment.

So it takes skill to navigate. The development of a soul perspective in conjunction with the ability to focus attention is the basis of that skill. With that skill, we can reach into experience for the particular sense of connection for which we yearn and the sense of purpose that fulfills our reason for being on the planet in the first place. Knowing is the intelligence by which we focus our attention with intention to experience our inherent connection with other. It is when we become One, one by one, while becoming the one who we are.

# 5

# THINKING: THE INTEGRATION
# OF EXPERIENCE

WHAT MAKES THINKING DIFFERENT than knowing?

Knowing is an immediate engagement with the world. It is non-verbal in its essence. It is raw and unpredictable. Knowing is where novelty resides. It is the fundamental process of *perception.*

Perception has to do with the act of sensing, feeling into, connecting with. Never mind that scientific thinking assumes that perception occurs in the brain. Some of it might happen there, but it occurs, in general, as a consequence of body senses distributed throughout the body, including the brain/mind. Immediate engagement with raw experience is its own *event*, prior to any labeling of that event by the thinking mind. It occurs across the entire range of the body's aware sensuality. Knowing is the body's highly developed sense, animated by the awareness of the observer soul, that forms the *intelligence of knowing.*

Thinking is the *intelligence of conception* that allows for the integration of experience. "Thinking" derives from a Latin source meaning to "take in." It is the process of abstracting or labeling the event of sensing. It is inherently language based upon and secondary to the act of perceiving.

Thinking also uses *preceptions,* which are language-based concepts embedded in the mind before a new *per*ception occurs.

It is thinking that precedes new experience. *Preception* is the pre-existing filter that frames raw experience at the outset—perhaps preventing it altogether. Preception certainly becomes part of the process of conception at the later time, following the event of raw experience, at which the mind's conception attempts to make meaning out of raw experience. With the presence of preception, thinking both precedes and follows raw experience.

Preception can include concepts that were created from one's prior experience, but it has come in modern usage to mean social rules established to govern the thinking and behavior of the individual in society, such as social concepts of morality and governmentally established laws—heavy-duty preceptions that say, "Don't even think about thinking otherwise." Religious laws are precepts. They are intended to *pre*vent even the temptation to have particular kinds of your own raw experience and to prevent you from judging your experience for yourself.

This is what I mean by the notion of filters. Our pre-extant thoughts tend to bias the process of forming new ideas from raw experience. And language itself is one huge pre-extant thought. Marshall McLuhan's insight was that "the medium is the message," as well as the "massage." If we are going to think in language, then we are predisposed to arrive at meanings already contained in the language used by the culture that has pre-existed our thinking process. It is very difficult to think outside a box made of thinking.

It is this very dilemma that has disposed Zen Buddhists to avoid naming experience. Rather, Zen suggests that we keep a "beginner's mind," one that is not already filled with concepts and precepts. Life is a continuing flow of experience. Do not name the experience, Zen teaches, since naming draws you out of the flow. I appreciate and admire this sentiment and the skillful attention practice that it emphasizes, but it makes it difficult to talk about meaning, including the particular category of meaning that I am calling soul purpose. Still, Zen emphasizes the value and importance of raw experience in its effort to bring us closer to our spiritual nature. I depart from Zen in this way: while raw experience is primary and central, naming and thinking provide the means of *integrating our new experience* into the flow of our lives in light of our histories and our need to change, heal, and find purpose.

Knowing tells us where to go. Thinking makes the reservations. If we do not make the mistake of thinking that thinking is more important than raw individual experience, we can see thinking and knowing as *complementary but different processes of equal value,* each necessary but neither sufficient to reach the level of intelligence necessary to navigate the world. To achieve the potential of the intelligence represented by the body's sensuality, raw sensation must *collaborate* with thinking. Knowing penetrates the mystery of our inherent connection and discovers the resonant pathway that pulls us toward a particular future. Thinking helps us move along that pathway. Knowing points out a direction. Thinking organizes the trip.

In a schematic way of speaking, one can speak of experience preceding thinking. But there is always thinking that preceded the new experience. The old thinking becomes part of the new experience. One can analogize to a *loop.* The old thinking and old experience become part and parcel of new experience, which fights for its place in what has preceded it.

Joseph Chilton Pearce, in his early writing, spoke of the experience of *metanoia:* a fundamental transformation of mind. For me, a combination of meditation, reading, Native American ceremony, and vision quests all created experience and concepts that *evolved* my mind even as my mind continued to reflect the heavy influences of early socialization. My metanoia occurred with the first ayahuasca ceremony. An older and terribly limited view of the world was shaken loose in hours, while raw experience filled my consciousness and waited years for a new and coherent worldview to take the place of the old.

This is one important aspect of Pearce's work. He has said, in essence, it is not enough to look at what the mind is doing in light of what it has done. The mind and brain are in a process of evolution. As the prefrontal cortex emerges, it changes the way in which the older brain structure works, even as the older brain created the supportive structure from which the prefrontal cortex emerged. And that evolution is finally a matter of whether there arises a coherence in the body/heart/mind that allows for the emergence of a whole new way of thinking that is dependent upon the full emergence of this new prefrontal cortex structure that we have already seen fully developed in some but not all humans. Its emergence relies upon the presence of love, first, from a secure and nurturing mother, second, from the earth, and, finally, from the ability to create a heart-based coherence in the body. Pearce does not speculate about souls. But he is quite open to the idea that fields of love are necessary to grow a body/mind that operates in love.

The highest human intelligence is one that is grounded in a fully operative prefrontal cortex naturally connected to a coherent heart that is connected to other coherent fields in the cosmos. My thesis is that a self-identified, focused, coherent soul leads us toward that potential.

Absent that achievement, there are less effective levels of thinking. If our raw experience arises from a body that has been traumatized, the body's thinking will be defensive and fear-based. That consequence arises from the common sequence of thought by which new experience is processed. Simply stated, we perceive a new event on our horizon. There is a change occurring, and we move to thinking immediately. Our thinking asks a question even before the new experience has unfolded: "Does this have anything to do with me?" Then the mind races into what is literally a life review, one that operates by analogy, or perhaps by simile. The mind asks: "What is this new experience like that I have experienced before?" If our history is one of trauma, then the prior experience of trauma sets the bias for interpretation of the new experience in terms of the old. We are predisposed by our conceptions of our prior experience—our preconceptions—to see the new experience as similar to the old.

HeartMath points to the amygdala, a small structure located centrally in the brain, which acts as a memory bank of all the body's experience. As the raw experience of the perception of the new event is making its way to the developing prefrontal cortex for what we hope to be some rational, heart-connected processing, the information that a new experience is coming passes through the amygdala. Quickly running through the file cards that represent prior experience, the amygdala senses for what the new experience *feels* like in terms of prior experience. Then it sends that information on to the cortex. So, as the prospect of new experience arrives at the cortex, before or as the new experience is actually processed by the cortex, our thinking is already colored by the emotional sense imprinted on the new by the old. In that way, the new experience is rather neatly boxed within the prior experience, and we are unable to meet the new experience in its raw state. If our prior experience has been challenging or painful, we naturally see any new experience in that light, assuming that it will be more of the same. So we raise our defenses even before we can taste what may be bringing the very connection and nurture for which we have yearned from behind our formidable defenses.

In theory, all that amygdala influence might seem like a good thing. The more experienced we are, the better able we are to meet what life throws at us. The problem arises when our life experience has resulted in trauma and we find ourselves unable to meet new experience without assuming or believing that the new experience—any new experience—portends more trauma. That is the reason that so many people, early in life, find themselves unable to open to new experience, deeply defended, unable to achieve intimacy, and totally blocked from the means of finding purpose.

Life, of course, is not all rose petals. We can philosophize that there are an equal number of thorns. But it really depends on how you look at it. One can learn to grasp the rose gently, connect with its beauty, smell its aroma, and recognize that the thorns serve to protect the rose from those who would consume it rather than connect with its beauty. Using this sort of analogy, we might stop to think that our trauma-based, amygdala-wired history could be shifted if we look at the engagement with the rose in a different way.

What HeartMath teaches is that the traumatic history stored in the amygdala can be circumvented and possibly rewired by creating coherence in the heart. Through heart coherence, the body's trauma-based view of the world can be shifted as the body begins to experience the sense of safety that comes with a coherent heart. Mae-Wan Ho's view is that the coherent heart can bring the body quickly—by its liquid crystalline nature—to a state of coherence that is experienced as what she calls a "mystical" experience. Beyond that, Ho suggests that the coherent body then has the capacity to resonate harmonically with those fields in nature that are also coherent, supporting and deepening the sense of connection between the body and nature that is sometimes the agent of a mystical experience.

What I teach is that the coherent soul—one that is self-identified, fully focused, and seated in the heart portal—cultivates coherence in the body by reaching beyond the body's prior experience and into the flow of experiences life offers day by day. With that reach, the soul can discover which experiences are to be embraced and which are to be avoided. It does so by the sense of resonance or dissonance that arises in the immediacy of raw experience as those possibilities appear on the *horizon* of experience. The horizon of experience, as this linguistic analogy implies, is as the light of the sun that chases away the night sky before the sun itself becomes visible and so bright that it prevents us from looking at it directly. We can taste what is coming by looking at and feeling into it with a *resonance based in coherence* rather than judgment based in a history of trauma held in the body that has hardwired fear into our brain.

Thinking is *intellect,* which is a component of but less than the whole of *intelligence.* Thinking is a process that we associate with the brain-mind, while knowing is a process we associate with the heart. Each requires the fundamental and underlying awareness that originates with the soul and shines its light through heart and mind alike. *Intellect* is the term we have come to make synonymous with *mind.* But intelligence is far more than mere intellect, more than mere manipulations of precepts and concepts in a field largely void of raw experiential percepts. The potential of intelligence is found in the collaboration of heart and mind in a field of coherence that overrides the limiting and fearful influence of filters, while rendering raw experience into new concepts by resonating with what is harmoniously coherent in a continually changing world.

You may have noticed that I have not described thinking in common terms of analysis, comparison, scrutiny, logic, rationality, and critical thinking. All of those are apt, but they fail to acknowledge the larger context within which the thinking mind can operate when it is liberated from its social limitation to precepts. Science and religion alike have denigrated personal experience as "merely" subjective and without significance. They say, in effect, what you think is not as valuable and important as what we think. Speaking directly to the angel amounts to heresy in scientific and religious circles alike.

What appears to me to be particularly pertinent about the nature of these common descriptions of what thinking is about is the basic process by which thinking happens. While knowing is a stepping into, thinking is a distinct stepping back. It is observation at a distance, whether it is with the telescope or microscope. Thinking is about taking things apart, crushing them between the glass slides, holding them in the flame, dissolving them in the medium—any way we can devise to see all the little parts.

As we put our eye to the microscope, we get a form of raw experience of our own thinking. We encounter a pre-existing concept that we are separate from this thing we have crushed between the glass slides. Something in our consciousness logically assumes that we also are separate from all the "objects" of the world toward which we direct our scrutiny. As we see ourselves as separate—and more importantly, *experience ourselves as separate*—we *feel* separate. And when we feel separate in a large world that we also see as complex and unyielding to our small individuality, with our amygdalae humming along, singing the blues to our cortices, our experience begins to loop around itself. We feel alone, vulnerable, exposed. That is the consequence of our addictive dependence upon thinking as a sole and sufficient process, whether we are deep thinkers or thinkers whose every thought is scratched out by a reptilian brain that has seized control from the moderate mammalian brain and the progressive prefrontal cortex, which is having trouble getting much attendance at its meetings. This is how things work in the absence of coherence.

When the heart reaches in and learns by becoming other, by feeling into that with which it connects, the opposite happens. There is a sense of being connected in the world, rather than separated from it. The body relaxes. The sense of connection creates a sense of safety. We can explore all the more.

To be sure, we get better "objective" information with the technology that is racing into our hands. Scientific exploration of the physiology of intelligence is moving forward more quickly now due to various technologies, including SQUID magnetometers, conventional ECG and EEG techniques, functional magnetic resonance imaging (fMRI), and polarizing light microscopy. SQUID technology has shown how quickly electromagnetic changes move across brain tissues. fMRI allows us to observe how the brain lights up in real time in response to particular kinds of experience. ECG and EEG allow pattern analysis of heart and brain rhythms. The polarizing microscope, as explained by biophysicist Mae-Wan Ho, allows the detection of "phase ordering" in the molecules of living organisms, which permits the observation of the presence of dynamic order or *coherence,* an analysis to which all of these technologies contribute. But, even with an ability to watch energy flow through particular brain structures or other body parts, we are not close to discovering the authoritative and proven "facts" that represent a comprehensive understanding of intelligence, where it comes from, how it works, or how to train it. Period.

The absence of a comprehensive understanding of intelligence is evident from even brief review of scientific theories of intelligence. We could start with Neo-Darwinian evolutionary theory, now seen by many as deeply inadequate to explain how humans have arrived at all, much less arrived at the distinctly human ability to think. Paul MacLean's idea of the evolution of a triune brain was a major influence in our thinking about how consciousness *operated* and perhaps evolved at the physical level of the body, but it did not answer in any way how consciousness *came to be.* Roger Sperry's theory about the lateralization of intelligence functions in the left and right brains won him the Nobel Prize in 1981 but has largely been put to the side as fMRI shows us a greater complexity of informational processing occurring bilaterally in the brain. Howard Gardner's theory of multiple intelligences, initially published in 1991, was certainly an innovation in the thinking about intelligence, but it did not transcend theory or even provide more than a new direction in thinking about intelligence, as Gardner himself acknowledged. Also in the 1990s, John Mayer, Peter Salovey, and Daniel Goleman brought the idea of emotional intelligence into our thinking, but their innovational work did not transcend theory either. Other work that has been important in the field of intelligence theory includes Candace Pert's description of neuropeptides, which galvanized the mind/body movement that has diffused our exclusive focus on the brain as the location of intelligence, while offering a concrete avenue of exploration of the connection of emotions to thinking.

Lesser-known but important contributors to our thinking about intelligence include Joseph Chilton Pearce, whom I've mention above. Pearce's life work brought him to describing the link between heart and brain as critical to understanding childhood development and intelligence. His work has linked various sources of research to explain how a mother's heart-based love is critical to the development of the prefrontal cortex. Central to Pearce's explorations is the work of Rollin McCraty of the HeartMath Institute. Also doing innovative research in the area of the heart-brain connection is Richard Davidson of the University of Wisconsin-Madison, whose work has used fMRI to observe the response of the brain to a heart-centered focus of attention by skilled Buddhist compassion meditators. And there is other relevant research that has not caught popular public attention. Austrian Alfred Pischinger's work—brought to American attention by James Oschman—addresses the connective tissue (or extracellular matrix) as a significant contributor to the mechanism of human intelligence. British biophysicist Mae-Wan Ho's work on quantum coherence, which connects with the HeartMath research, is perhaps most satisfying to my mind's desire for an explanation of how intelligence works in the body.

Some simple facts are quite apparent from the review of this recent history of the scientific exploration of intelligence: we understand very little of the mystery of the body, its intelligence, or its mechanism of intelligence; and science is unable to address the subject of consciousness in any significant way other than to acknowledge that it must exist. Mainstream science is deeply limited by both its inability and its frequent unwillingness to approach consciousness as a phenomenon distinct from the physical matter through which it operates.

To be clear, it is not my intention to suggest a *theory* of intelligence. Nor am I trying to be factual. Suggesting that we label our individual attention a distillation of the whole of consciousness and calling it by the name of *soul* doesn't make my explanation a theory. I'm not trying to prove anything or propose a scientific theory suitable for the investigation of a hypothesis by scientific methodology, although you can experiment with what I'm saying at the level of personal experience. But it is not what science would regard, in its so-called objective methodology, as an experiment. Your experiment can be your science, using the methodology of subjectivity, which is no more or less than raw experience. I am suggesting an understanding of *my experience* of intelligence, in all the scientific insufficiency that understandings inevitably represent. That is entirely different. I'm saying, in effect, this is how we can engage intelligence experientially, in a larger personal way than our very limited scientific thinking can access and without having to fully understand it. And without being able to understand it, we can nevertheless *know* it. And, with this more simplistic approach, we can see that there are three primary categories of human intelligence: knowing, thinking, and visioning.

Let's look at visioning next.

# 6

# VISIONING: THE POSSIBILITY
# OF EXPERIENCE

I HAVE HAD MANY VISIONS.

The first I recall was when I was eleven years old. My elder sister had left for college, leaving me the attic bedroom that had been the domain of both my older sisters. As I made it my own, arranged the furniture to suit, and settled at my little desk with pen and paper, I had an image of myself sitting in a circular room in which the walls were covered with filled bookcases. I saw myself in the center of the room, writing.

Forty years later, with the advent of my relationship with plant medicines, visions became a more commonplace event for me. But, almost four years after my initial encounter with ayahuasca, I experienced a crystal clear vision quite without the plant medicine. It occurred during a ceremonial initiation called, in the Peruvian Q'ero tradition, a *kawak*. The initiation occurred in a shamanic workshop on an afternoon when a nap was more likely. I've wondered whether the earlier experience with ayahuasca might have opened a channel that something came through years later, but I have no answer for that.

I told the story of this particular vision in *The Soul's Critical Path*. I called it the vision of the *inner marriage,* and it continued over a period of thirty days, weaving in and out of my daily meditation. As I stepped back to look at and write about it, I eventually concluded that it was a comprehensive look at the then current relationship between my inner masculine and feminine, followed by a sequence of events that prepared me for the healing of those elements. The vision ended with the feminine and masculine figures in the vision kneeling before an altar. The altar was situated on an energy bridge between two Peruvian mountains— sacred mountains regarded in that tradition as *apus,* or fifth-dimensional spirit beings. Behind the altar were four elders, two men and two women, all of whom had participated in the healings and trainings that were part of the vision that had preceded this moment. It was apparent that there was going to be a marriage. To my surprise, as the vision ended, there was no marriage. I had, I concluded later, been provided with a healing template that I could walk into, or not.

In 2015, in a plant medicine ceremony, I had a vision that completed this earlier vision. I experienced the consummation of the potential of the first and realized that the marriage had finally occurred. Over eleven years, there had been considerable personal work that made the potential into a reality. The primary vision had provided the pathway and the map.

I've already mentioned the vision that occurred during the deathbed psychodrama, which occurred months before the vision of the inner marriage. Again, no plant medicines were involved. Years later, in 2013, a series of visions began that related to a particular temple in Peru that is associated with the 3,000-year-old Chavin culture. The vision, like that of the inner marriage, occurred and recurred in serial fashion over many weeks, then over many months, arising without warning in my meditation. Again, it provided a combination of information, healing, and initiation.

These visionary experiences have been clear and compelling, and I continue to have them from time to time. Each has been influential in shaping both my understanding of the world and my place in it.

But I am quite unsure what a vision is. Obviously, they have come in different ways and in different circumstances.

Brain research seems to affirm that the left hemisphere is dominant for language, logic, mathematics, and rote learning. The right hemisphere is dominant for visual-spatial ability and the ability to make and respond to music, although particular elements of music—pitch, melody, and tempo—involve the left hemisphere. At the same time, the brain has an ability, sometimes called "plasticity," that allows for a certain degree of function shifting if that becomes necessary. I mention this laterality of the brain only to suggest that what little we know of brain physiology suggests a division of labor that corresponds to our direct experience that processing language with logic, for example, has a distinctly different feel to it than day-dreaming, for any value of what a day-dream may represent. Because music evokes activity in the same hemisphere that is active with visioning, I keep my piano keyboard just a few feet away from my computer keyboard. It helps me keep mental balance to shift back and forth from writing to the kind of dream state that allows for vision, and my improvising for a few minutes on the piano seems to move me toward that door.

Simply stated, visual-spatial ability allows us to see figures in two and three dimensions. My ayahuasca visions have certainly been three-dimensional. We take this mystery of vision, both external and internal, for granted because it is so common. Yet science has little understanding of sight beyond its observation of the phenomenon of externally sourced light alighting upon the structures of the eye, which can then be followed along neurological pathways that ultimately register regionally in the brain, where images are produced that seem projected out before our bodies.

Internal vision, however, remains an acknowledged mystery. It would seem—at least to the casual observer—that it is dark inside the body. Mae-Wan Ho and ayahuasca researcher Jeremy Narby, among others, speak of photon activity occurring throughout the body. Still, it is difficult for me to imagine those photons creating the starkly brilliant luminescence that has characterized some of my visions—appearing like multicolored fluorescent geometries in full motion or fully illuminated figures both humanlike and quite otherwise. Other visions have been less stark in their brilliance, but clear and in full color nevertheless. On most of those occasions, there has been an auditory aspect in which the vision is accompanied by a voice apprehended—I hesitate to say "heard"—internally.

I don't need to understand how this clair-audience might occur to be content that I *know it exists*. My sense that these events have their own reality—in which I experienced myself as an active observer and participant—remains quite unshakable.

My visions seem like waking dreams, similar to but distinct from the dreams of our sleeping state. Just as sleeping dreams may be alternately crystal clear, indistinct, or fleeting to the inner eye, so may the visions that enter our waking consciousness be more clear or less. And the subject or significance of the waking dream may be no different than what is accessed by the sleeping dream, having little significance or great. Certainly, the literature of human experience recounts significant information imparted to sleeping dreamers. And there is certainly the suggestion that the quality of information available to a sleeping dreamer can be enhanced with intention and technique. While I have experienced a few archetypal sleeping dreams, none have approached the length, depth, and intensity of my waking visions.

For the purpose of what I want to say about vision in this book, my foundational understanding of visions is very conventional and may seem obvious: the ability to see is not the same as thinking. Perhaps it is only obvious if you have both the ability to think and the ability to experience the internal seeing that visions seem to be. Looking out upon the world is a form of raw experience in and of itself. Thinking seems to be a secondary processing of primary raw experience, until it is the thought itself that becomes the raw experience to the soul's observation. For me, internal vision is also a form of raw experience. At the same time, it is also a form of processing of experience. Let me see if I can explain.

The analysis, comparison, scrutiny, logic, and rationality that characterize critical thinking have certain *reductive* qualities. We strain to see a thing or a fact in its most essential, but nevertheless conceptual, expression. What is an atom? Is it parts? What are the parts? We keep finding more. How do they behave? We continue tuning our microscopes more finely to answer such questions.

What I am calling *vision* is perhaps the opposite. With vision we can see parts but can also see parts operating together. We can see a big picture. We are able see a *system* rather than a component. Vision can be a holistic way of seeing. It is a *relational* way of seeing. Rather than isolating a feature for separate analysis, vision is a gathering of everything that is connected with an opportunity to see the connections as an operating whole. While thinking can be systemic, the visioning of a whole underwrites thinking's ability to shift to a greater systemic wholeness.

Still, both thinking and visioning involve a certain disengagement with the object of observation. With thinking, we separate ourselves from the isolated "object" of observation in order to see its particular nature. With visioning, we separate ourselves from the collectivity of objects to see them in systemic relationship.

This stepping back to observe is just the opposite of how the heart works, which is to move into, to connect with, to merge with, and to know. The heart provides raw experience. With the heart, we can move through our inherent connection with the all to know the nature of the individuated as well as the collective. And, with the heart, we can move into our own singular thoughts, as well as our own visions, to know our own thoughts and visions from the inside out.

In a general sense, I think of visioning in its mundane, ordinary sense as the simple ability to grasp the big picture. Few people seem capable of that, perhaps because of a cultural conditioning to and contentment with the accessibility of thinking as a default mode, particularly as thinking becomes the host for the imported beliefs that mimic the organic thinking that arises from one's own knowing and visioning. In American culture, for example, it has become easier to participate in political dialogue by focusing on one or two beliefs—such as the absolute right to own an AR-15 and the evil of abortion—rather than seeing how those beliefs actually operate in the big picture of social life.

# 7

# EXPANDED THINKING AND VISIONING

## The Mind's Eye

THERE IS ANOTHER QUALITY of visioning commonly associated with spiritual work that happens as a consequence of skill development but does not necessitate operating through the heart portal to access the body's sensuality. This other way uses the more familiar portal that is often called the *third eye.*

The soul may access and use the third eye without regard for the heart portal at all for the reason that the third eye is available to the soul even though the soul may not have an optimal relationship with the body. The third eye is a common way for the soul to access other dimensions. The form of this access is not merger with the objects and opportunities of the world. The sight accessed through the third eye is also a step removed from its object. The difference is that third eyesight is focused upon other dimensions.

This distinction is one that I am helped to understand by the skillful work of my life partner, Darlene Joy, who is clairvoyant. As I have watched her work and discussed with her our respective experiences, I have gradually come to a provisional understanding that one can travel out of the body through the third eye; that it is the soul that travels; that such travel can occur solely by use of the third eye or in combination with the heart portal; and that the singular use of either portal is different than using them in combination. Over time, it is my understanding that Darlene's gift is a natural and easy access to the third eye portal. But, as she has demonstrated in the trajectory of her personal work, bringing that capacity into a greater relationship with the heart has enhanced both her ability and the value of her work on behalf of her clients.

The Q'ero tradition of southern Peru that is commonly associated most directly with the Inca tradition shares an initiation called the *kawak,* the same ceremony I mentioned in the prior chapter. The kawak directly addresses this combination of the two portals. Using stones to trace energetic pathways, the Q'ero connect the third eye, the occipital vision area of the brain, and the heart. Q'ero healers do so by using the stones to trace the pathway of the vagus nerve that connects the three areas. The Q'ero explain that it is critical to connect the capacity of the third eye to access other dimensions with both the physical capacity for sight and the heart itself. Without connecting the heart to the third eye, I have understood the Q'ero to say, the information accessed through the third eye will not be reliable. If I were to speculate upon the reason why, I would suggest that the heart lends the condition of coherence to the inquiry of the third eye, so that there is both a merger and a one-step-removed vision that combine for a deeper level of personal truth. When we see with our eyes, including our third eye, we have a deeper opportunity for discernment when we also feel into what we see with our hearts.

When I access my own vision, I do so with the intention to approach the third eye through my heart. Nevertheless, it is the third eye that gives greater power to the knowing that happens when we use the heart alone. It is as if the vision illustrates our knowing, and our knowing grounds our vision. This is as good an example of the collaboration of intelligences of heart and vision as I can imagine. The further collaboration with the thinking intelligence provides for the integration of that deeper experience into the big picture understandings by which we plan our pathways forward.

If people do not have the capacity to see the big picture, it is not because they lack the opportunity to do so. The body seems quite designed to permit such vision. Whether we access that capacity depends upon whether we are willing and motivated to develop the *skill* of visioning in collaboration with the heart skill of knowing. The skill consists of the combination of bringing soul to its fully focused state, seating the soul in its home away from home in the heart portal, bringing the body to the soul-receptive state that requires a soul-facilitated sense of safety in the body, and bringing the soul's attention to the world through the body's sensuality or its third eye.

## The Mind's Ear

Just as our capacity for knowing can work through the body's sensuality, in general, and its visionary capacity, in particular—what we might call the *mind's eye*—so can the capacity for knowing extend itself through the *mind's ear*.

I have had this experience in two ways.

First, I have found my poetry to arise in a way that my prose does not, or at least to the same degree. My prose involves far more ordinary thinking—the processing of the raw experiences of visioning or knowing into language. My poetry doesn't seem to work that way. Instead, often as I am meditating, an insight will arrive directly in language. I will "hear" a phrase. The phrase seems particularly apt, by which I mean that the language catches a metaphor that communicates a thought strongly, in a way that the meaning behind the metaphor is likely to be communicated simply and effectively. For example, in my prose, I have written at length about the difference between fate and destiny. Speaking poetically, I have said that fate is lemons; destiny is lemonade. Clear enough?

And the apt phrase has a tail or, perhaps, a tale. There are more words attached. If I race to my computer, I'll find that the phrase may turn into an entire poem. If a poem is actually "happening" to me, then the words pour out without any effort or analysis on my part. It doesn't have the more eye-squinting, concentrating feel of intellectual analysis that is involved in creating an understanding from experience. It either comes or it doesn't. If I have to work at it, it isn't happening. If I begin to feel that I'm having to figure it out, I just stop—settling for the recognition that I missed the opportunity to "hear" the flow of words. The words seem to be coming from somewhere else. When they do, it feels quite different than when they come from my own thinking.

My understanding of the difference is that there are other-dimensional fields of intelligence that inform our heart knowings, our visionings, and also our linguistic thinking, all independent of the ordinary use of each of these capacities. What is clear to me is that this greater reach is a function either of a natural gift or of the more sweaty work of skill development. The skill development is, once more, focusing the soul, getting it seated in the heart, and amplifying the sensuality of the body until the ears and eyes cross dimensional lines.

The second way my mind's ear has revealed itself is during vision quests. I wrote about these in *The Soul's Critical Path.* During the 1990s, I did a number of quests that involved my picking a remote spot in nature where I could be largely undisturbed by people and where nature itself was relatively undisturbed by noise, pollution, or EM waves. For six days, I would remain in isolation in a circle not exceeding 100 meters in diameter. My method was to do nothing but remain present. I would support myself with meditation and qigong while fasting on tea and fruit juice made by placing two jars in the sun each day. During each of six such quests, I heard a low drone sound throughout the entire time, growing in intensity from the beginning until the end of the time.

On two occasions, in 1995 and 2000, there was another sound that arose, so to say, out of the drone sound. Both sounds turned out to be Hindu mantras that I had never heard before, although I had used other mantras in my meditation practice over several prior years. Both mantras came complete with rhythm and rhythmic tonal shifts, or music. After the second incident, I was able to share the mantras with Pandit Rajmani Tiganut, then director of the Himalayan Institute, to inquire whether the sounds I heard were indeed among the traditional mantras of the Vedic tradition. He confirmed that they were.

Since I had no other way of knowing these mantras, my only possible understanding is that they came full blown—language, music, and all—directly into my mind. Since there was no materialistic explanation for their source, I can only presume that their source was other-dimensional. On both occasions, my routine practice also involved the chanting of the well-known *gayatri* mantra three times daily during the quest. Both events occurred before I started a heart-centered meditation practice. So it makes some sense that I had tuned my attention to a particular set of other-dimensional fields of intelligence. Certainly, this is not a factual conclusion, but it is as good a provisional understanding as I have been able to manage.

With that understanding, it seems clear to me that the mind/brain has ordinary thinking and visioning capacities and that it also has further capacities that are skill activated. Bringing these into a fully intentional collaboration with a soul focus grounded in the heart's capacity for knowing is precisely the pathway to discover soul purpose. There is a great deal of help in this intentional cosmos for the unveiling of who you are and why you are here.

How that is done with a simplified process is the subject of Part Four, and it requires that we first overcome the deleterious and damaging effect of belief, which is the subject of Part Three, next.

PART THREE

# WHAT RESISTS IT:
# BREAKING WITH BELIEF

# INTRODUCTION TO
# PART THREE

## Breaking with Belief

WESTERN CULTURE BELIEVES IN BELIEF. In the course of learning how to strengthen my soul and ground my soul purpose on the planet, I found Western culture's embrace of belief to be hostile. Western *religious* culture, in particular, has fostered a belief in belief. Ironically, scientific culture has supported religious culture in this respect. As I realized an inherent inconsistency between belief and personal experience, I found myself having to break with belief altogether. Part Three explains why.

I will suggest that the discovery of soul purpose and the means of grounding it on a changing planet are absolutely dependent upon a process of personal experience. In the chapters that follow, I will show how the Catholic Church made a strategic decision in its early years to prohibit a process of personal experience and mandate a process of belief as the sole means of connection with God. That decision has permeated our cultural thinking, including non-religious thinking, ever since.

It is often enough said that the United States has lost its soul. This is why.

# *Defining Belief*

There are three meanings that can be associated with the word "belief." The word is commonly used to define a concept adopted as inherently true even though it is not susceptible of proof either by scientific means or direct personal experience.

Take, for example, the statement "I believe in the divinity of Lord Jesus Christ." Accepting the meaning given to the statement by mainstream Christianity, we can say with some confidence that scientific method does not lend itself to supporting or dispelling such truth claims.

As an alternative example, consider the statement "I believe in Jesus." Historical investigation reveals a small amount of evidence for the existence of a man of Galilee whose probable social circumstances were consistent with some of the biblical stories attributed to such a man. But that use of "belief" can be quite different from the meaning most probably intended by "I believe in the divinity of Lord Jesus Christ." If I were to use the phrase "I believe in Jesus," my meaning could be more accurately conveyed by saying, "I understand that the man we call Jesus probably lived, that he probably lived in Galilee, and that he may have become the impetus for the stories that became the foundation for modern Christianity." In this latter usage, belief means what I use the word "understand" to convey.

So, sometimes we use the word "belief" to refer to what we think without regard for a preliminary personal experience and for which there is no scientific evidence. Sometimes we use it to refer to an understanding based upon scientific evidence or scholarly research and analysis. Similar to the difference between theory and fact, there is a difference between these two usages of belief.

While it is common to use the words "understand" and "believe" as having the same meaning, we would never say "I believe in apples." Neither belief nor understanding refers to direct perceptions. We can directly perceive an apple hanging in the tree, take it in hand, and put it in our mouths. We can *know* an apple and bring that knowing into a conceptual and linguistic understanding that is one step removed from the experience beneath the tree. But belief, in the narrow sense of talking about an idea or concept we embrace as true despite the *absence* of the direct perception of personal experience, has no application to an apple we have eaten.

With Jesus, I can have no direct personal experience because I cannot see him or take him in hand. Putting the wafer in my mouth does not remedy this absence. I can read about Jesus, fully dependent upon the intervening perceptions of others who might have recorded what they had seen or heard. I can read the work of a number of scholars to see whether a consensus among scholars of good reputation exists or is trending relative to the historical record. I can assess for myself what level of consensus and repu-tation are sufficient indicators of reliability. While I can adopt an understanding based upon my assessment of the reliability of those accounts, my understanding in such a case would remain *provisional*. Being provisional, my understanding remains always subject to revision based upon more reliable accounts and the discovery of new evidence for parsing by "experts." But forming valuable understandings from the work of such scholars requires that we become "almost scholars" ourselves.

So there are three meanings to the notion of belief. First, there is the embrace of a concept for which there is no evidence. Second, there is a provisional understanding based upon credible perceptions made by others using some scientific or scholarly methodology. And third, there is a provisional understanding aris-ing from the personal experience of knowing.

I have broken from the first of these, which I'll restate here: *a truth claim that is not a provisional understanding derived from raw personal experience, reliable scholarship, or the application of scientific method.*

## Why We Rely on Belief

One can quickly find many reasons we might favor belief, whether we think of it as a process or not.

First, we haven't made the mental effort to carefully distinguish in our ordinary speech the difference between belief and a provisional understanding.

Second, we want to understand what is going on in the world around us, but there is too much information to digest, analyze, and understand even provisionally. Even if we were to delegate the task to specialists, our education has not provided many of us with the "almost scholars" capacity to assess or even follow what the professional scholars and scientists debate. So, without the skill of heart-based knowings, we resort to belief.

Third, an apparent majority of honest scientists who acknowledge the limitations of scientific method have also acknowledged belief as a proper subject for religion, which has embraced the process of belief. Despite the tension between science and religion, the two sides of this divide basically defer to each other as *legitimate* purveyors of what they purvey in their respective domains. There are dissenters, to be sure. For the most part, however, religion and science are accepted as the only legitimate validators of truth, for different values of "truth."

Fourth, those dissenters—atheistic scientists among them (you can Google the list)—essentially direct their criticism toward the *content* of what the believers believe rather than upon the process of belief itself. They do so because they embrace the process of belief for themselves, denying the existence of a mystery to which they cannot connect and which they cannot disprove. They confuse absence of evidence for evidence of absence.

Fifth, some dissenters have even said that belief, despite what they claim to be its fallacious content, might be a good thing because it helps people feel safer in a fearful world. So we believe, atheists and religious alike, because it feels better.

Sixth, we can see that the common sources of "knowledge" that stand beyond belief aren't inherently reliable when we actually lift the lid. Some scientists accept money to construct false conclusions in what masquerades as a legitimate study, while studies of scientific studies are showing that a significant percentage of studies are inherently unreliable. At the same time, the evidence grows that the Church is built upon an intentional fabrication. So it is difficult to know, as a merely intellectual matter, what is factual or true as we navigate the complexity of life without or even with that "almost scholars" level of work. So belief becomes a default modality for those who don't know how to remain in a state of "don't know" as they work toward the experience of knowing.

# The Error of Science

The story of the emergence of science from the shadow of the Catholic Church is familiar, as are its primary characters, Nicolaus Copernicus and his later defender, Galileo Galilei. Copernicus died before the Church realized the implication of his work. Galileo, who confirmed Copernicus's theories with the technology of the telescope, was tried for his crime by the Church and confined to house arrest until his death. Much has been written about the emergence of scientific process from the tyranny of the Church. But one implication of that shift is clear without the necessity of revisiting that literature in detail: the rise of science was a challenge not only to the Church's claim of divine authority to define beliefs, but also to the Church's position that belief grounded in ecclesiastical authority should control what humans could know.

Copernicus and Galileo forwarded the notion that knowledge should instead be grounded in methodical observation of the material world, a process that came to be known as *empiricism.* Although couched in such language, scientific method is a form of the process of personal experience. Observation of the material world, whatever else it is or isn't, is about experience, not belief.

As science transcended the limitations of ordinary human senses with technological advances, from telescopes to microscopes, the reach of human experience grew rapidly. Even then, as science developed a power parallel to that of the Church, the reach of science has remained entirely in the *material* realm. To a large degree, science and religion have achieved a practical division of labor: religion gets the spiritual realm and the work of salvation, while science presides over the material realm and the work of creation. There is money to be made on both sides.

The foundational belief of science—and it is belief—is that observation of the external, material world provides "objective" information free of the inherent unreliability of untested beliefs, whether based in religious authority or in the subjective, internal world of personal experience. Even "scientific" observations that cannot be replicated by others are not regarded as reliable. So scientific process sets up a distinction between two kinds of personal experience, one asserted to be a valid indicator of fact-truth, and the other not. Science tells us that the *replicable* experience (therefore, not merely *individual* experience) of methodical observation provides reliable *facts*.

Even as science and Christianity seem otherwise pitted against each other, science's claim of the primacy of objective experience has found common ground with Christianity relative to the value of individual experience. Both minimize, denigrate, or dismiss any truth-value relative to subjective, internal experience. This common ground ultimately gave science something to give back to religion, either by way of establishing a truce or by the arrogant assumption that belief was irrelevant anyway. What was given up in that process was the realm of individual freedom to define one's own path in the world with that powerful capacity I have called *knowing*.

The error of science was and is to give the process of belief over to religion while failing to give knowing its own domain separate from the belief process of religion. Had it been otherwise, we might be in a different situation than we now find ourselves. Religious wars fueled by belief have rekindled and grown more dangerous in the time of technology, and none of us may survive that. Climate change scientists have certainly discovered the error of science's prior validation of belief as a legitimate process. It is coming back to bite them, and the rest of us as well. Belief is pushing climate science to the side.

# The Now Apparent Problem

While I will address the problem created for individual souls by the belief process in the following chapters, it is already apparent how the process of belief has created a significant problem within mainstream science and the soul of culture as a whole.

The broader problem is that belief has flooded beyond its accepted banks. Belief now subsumes the legitimate domain of science for an uneducated demographic that cannot or is unwilling to understand the difference between scientific and religious domains. In a culture where belief is widely accepted, it is now acceptable to use belief to negate clearly valid scientific positions. It is acceptable, for example, for a large portion of our American population to deny climate change is happening, or happening at the hands of humans, because it is acceptable to believe what we want to believe, without regard for strong scientific evidence to the contrary. It is apparent, for example, in the ambiguity that arises from our using the same word—*belief*—to refer to the conclusions of both science and religion, as when we say, "I believe in climate change," and "I believe in God."

There is a significant portion of our population that has the ability to engage with social media but cannot or is unwilling to distinguish a belief from a provisional understanding. Social media has allowed nonsense to become self-validating by the simple mechanism of broad dissemination of demagoguery that gives cover to all sorts of absurd beliefs. In that circumstance, it becomes entirely acceptable and self-validating to say, "I don't believe in climate change," or "Obama is a Muslim." With the same logic and linguistic usage, people are now saying, against the evidence and in an amazing act of non-self-reflection, that Christians want only the good, and Muslims are violent. We have come to a juncture in our cultural ignorance where belief is legitimate as a currency of truth on its own without regard to the domain to which science consigned it. Science put belief in the box of religion, and technology opened it back up. We can easily perceive that this belief in belief is taking us straight toward more war right in the midst of where climate change denial has already taken us.

With the advent of the Internet, social media, and the cult of Fox News, it is now possible to find a form of religious community outside of the Church. The community of believers no longer needs to congregate in a Church when it is possible to do so throughout the week in virtual groups. So, while the Church's historical position as the primary provider of community is arguably weakened in this way, the phenomenon of belief is strengthened. Belief is affirmed as a way to find community entirely outside of the previously most available opportunities provided by religion. Now, there are virtual communities available through the NRA, the Republican Party, Fox News, and the news sources that pander to our susceptibility to belief.

We find ourselves in this anomalous position because neither science nor religion "believes" in *personal experience* as a legitimate arbiter of truth or understandings. Science asserts personal experience to have less value, if any at all, compared to the "facts" produced by its own methods. The Catholic Church, for its part, long ago declared personal experience to be heresy, a position it maintains today. Membership in the Church *requires* that I adopt the process of belief and drop the process of personal experience.

As a consequence, *belief in belief* as a legitimate and valuable process of defining relationship between the individual and the cosmos remains strong and increasingly dominant in an increasingly uneducated modern culture.

And that belief is the greatest impediment to discovering your soul purpose, which is entirely dependent upon personal experience.

So, why do we believe so ardently in belief? Let's look more deeply, through the eyes of religious scholar Elaine Pagels, at how deeply the Catholic Church has committed our culture to the process of belief. Her study of the so-called gnostic gospels has, alongside the work of a few other scholars, opened a window into a debate that even much of the modern religious community does not remember. Because this happened at a time in history more than 1,500 years ago and we are not a culture much interested in history, the Church's strategic actions might have disappeared into a modern reality we have taken for granted as how things work. But things did not, and do not, have to work this way. Perhaps, with the insight provided by this excellent scholarship, you can find how deeply the process of belief has been implanted in your own psyche.

# 8

# THE GNOSTIC GOSPELS

IN 1945, SCROLLS WERE UNEARTHED near Nag Hammadi in Egypt. These documents have come to be called the "gnostic gospels," although some scholars now question whether that is the most accurate way to describe the entire body of work since these "gospels" also hint at perspectives that predate the Christian era. Nevertheless, the translations offer a previously unavailable insight to the times during which Christianity was forming and to the thinking that ultimately formed the Catholic Church. Elaine Pagels's thorough comparison of these scrolls to the biblical record and other available historical documents makes it abundantly clear that the path to establishment of the Church was fraught with a degree of disagreement not previously so apparent to either religious scholars or current-day true believers.

Early "Christians" disagreed upon the details of Jesus's life, his inherent divinity, what he did, what he said, and what his sayings meant. There was disagreement on the necessity of an organized, universal church. As time passed, there were competing interpretations of the Genesis story of Adam and Eve and its implications for moral freedom of choice and personal responsibility. There were different views on what it should take to become a Christian, as well as what becoming a Christian ultimately implied. And the so-called gnostic gospels reflect a clear divide on the question whether the embrace of belief alone was a sufficient basis for becoming a Christian, as opposed to a skilled process by which one could develop a direct, experiential relationship with God.

During the fourth century CE, the faction that ultimately prevailed in capturing the Christian movement into the emerging Catholic Church declared a direct and personal relationship with God as heresy. The conversion of the Roman emperor Constantine the Great brought the golden patronage of Rome to the emerging Church, providing the critical financial support that underwrote its future success. That financial support not only gilded the door that opened more widely to sincere believers, but attracted others who cared less about salvation than the opportunity to acquire power and wealth. And during the fifth century, St. Augustine of Hippo—then a bishop of the newly minted Catholic Church—came into even closer alignment with Rome in order to win a hotly contested theological argument that finally established *belief* as the defining process by which one both *became* a Christian and *practiced* Christianity. It was Augustine who single-handedly defined the Church's teaching on original sin, casting a shadow so long that we experience its darkness today.

What defined Christian religion for the next millennium and a half was not merely the considerable support of government and the exclusive content of its beliefs, but the *process* of belief itself. The losers' argument for a process of personal experience as a means of connecting with God was pushed aside. Without the insights provided by the scholarly analysis of the gnostic gospels, the existence of this debate might have been lost to history.

There are many different Christianities that come into view from the work of Pagels and other religious historians who have translated and analyzed the gnostic gospels. What these scholars show us is that the Christianity of today formed up at the expense of other possibilities and that the churches with which we are familiar now were an eventuality rather than an inevitability. However we may view the reality of the historical Jesus or the essential wisdom of the various messages attributed to him, it is clear that Jesus did not form the Catholic Church. The

Church formed Jesus. And it is this same Catholic Church and its Protestant progeny with which we live today, embedded deeply in the unconsciously held experiences of our bodies.

Pagels emphasizes that Augustine's interpretation of the Genesis *story* of Adam and Eve took a central role in that fateful historical debate. Surely, the founders of the Catholic Church recognized what debaters and writers know—that stories and the images they create are more persuasive than dry analysis and reason. Prominent among the beliefs crafted from the Genesis story by the emerging Church was Augustine's argument that humans were inevitably crippled by original sin and therefore incapable of making morally responsible choices. Modern Christianity's view remains that the sin of Adam and Eve resulted in the loss of human freedom to make choices in the moral realm apart from a single choice: join the Church and gain salvation of the soul at death, or don't and suffer eternal damnation. Among those who lost the debate on the issue of moral freedom and the question of how the Church should take form, there was a different view: turn inward, discover who you are, find a direct connection with God, and you will be able to make responsible moral choices during your lifetime. But the latter view did not prevail in the process of church making, even if it was not extinguished in the larger realm of human spirituality.

What is the core message of the Christianity that prevailed? My paraphrased summary of the position of the Church from then until now would be this: Profess these beliefs, says the Christian religion of the Apostles' Creed, and you may enter into the embrace of the Church. We will assist you in controlling the persistently sinful nature of the body against the ubiquity of temptations in the material world to which your soul has been condemned by the sins of original man and woman. We will arrange forgiveness of your sins and assure the salvation of your soul when you die. We will offer a community of support. We will greet your births and preside over your deaths. Suffering and death itself are the inevitable consequences of your inherently sinful nature, but prayer will help you endure until the soul can return to the heaven that original sin denies to humans who do not seek salvation through Christ and his Church. Have faith, and it will all come together in the end. A Catholic does not pick and choose. Indeed, to choose is heresy, because humans do not have the capacity for making individual moral choices.

These beliefs and the process of belief itself came as a package deal. And these are not simply the views of the Catholic Church. The Protestant churches that split from the Catholic Church did not fall far from the tree, and the reasons for the splits were not these bedrock positions.

These positions aren't selling well to current generations with a greater embrace of science, a taste for free expression of individuality, a sense of individual purpose, a view that sex is perhaps not sinful after all, a belief in personal choice, and a lower tolerance for suffering, delayed gratification, and hypocrisy. But Christianity has often been the only spiritual game in town, at least in the West. These Churches have provided a community for a broad range of believers that no other Western social mechanism has matched, and community has been critical to the survival of individual humans. All comers are welcome, so long as they do not overtly question the beliefs or bring their own out of the closet.

As politics, religion is pretty local. Good and wise priests and pastors have softened the message to keep pew and plate as full as possible, quietly making the congregation more inclusive, keeping some tangible social service on the table, keeping the nuns upon whose backs the Church has long stood from rebelling, and delivering on the promise of a supportive community. As I write, Pope Francis continues to soften the message, while his speeches are getting record crowds around the world. But I have not heard him indicate that the process of belief and apostolic authority upon which the Church were founded are up for negotiation. Personal experience has not been invited to commune at the Church's table.

From Pagels's analysis, I can discern four critical periods in the development of the Catholic Church: the proliferation of competing versions of stories told about Jesus during the first century following the time attributed to his death; the competition for control of the story as the Church was developing during the second and third centuries; the conversion of Constantine to Christianity in the third century, accompanied by his active support in financing and consolidating the Christian movement; and the incredibly dark imprint of Augustine, who prevailed over competing Christian views supporting the doctrine of free will. Augustine's legacy was to cement belief as the Church's singular process, to align the Church's mission with Rome's need to control a diverse population, and to write an interpretation of the Genesis story that created the largest possible net for converts while condemning them to a life of suffering.

Amidst these events emerged two strategies that were central to the formation and survival of the Church. One was the adoption of the process of belief and the rejection of the process of personal experience. The second was the creation of a broadly inclusive community that spoke effectively to the human need to belong. These developmental periods and strategies are the themes that I will address as I provide a sketch of Pagels's scholarly analysis in Chapter Nine.

I will draw upon three of Pagels's books as I explore these issues: *The Gnostic Gospels; Adam, Eve, and the Serpent;* and *Beyond Belief: The Secret Gospel of Thomas.*[23] I would refer my readers to the books themselves to draw their own conclusions from Pagels's work. I have selected those parts of her analysis that relate to the role of the *process* of belief, which Pagels did not describe as such. Pagels demonstrated the difference in the *content* of early beliefs that illuminated the contentious history of the Church's formation. What spoke to me between the lines of Pagels's commentary was how the winners fused content with process in a way that would have been impossible to untangle in modern times without the discovery of the gnostic gospels. The winners of the battle for the Church not only wrote the history that affirmed their position, but ordered the losers' histories burned.

What Pagels drew from her own analysis was that the gnostic gospels made certain critical content of Christian beliefs unbelievable, leaving her to seek on her own even as she expressed a continuing connection to the community of the Church from which she had found personal support in times of particular difficulty. In *Beyond Belief,* she did not break with belief as a process, but suggested a process of seeking based in a faith, possibly including beliefs, that would transcend reliance upon the discredited beliefs. In Chapter Ten, I will address Pagels's conclusion about the significance of the discrediting of the core beliefs of the Catholic Church for her as a Christian. I believe her own scholarship is open to an entirely different interpretation that is equally spiritual, but not religious—if "religious" is to be reserved for those who continue to seek with some combination of belief and faith.

I deeply honor Pagels's scholarship and accept as credible the facts—as reasonable provisional understandings—her scholarship has revealed. I respect that she clearly separates those scholarly understandings from her interpretation of the personal implication of these understandings for herself as a Christian. In Chapter Ten, however, I will suggest that a quite different understanding of the implication of her work is possible. I will suggest that the emphasis be given not to the content, but to the process of belief itself. I would argue that Pagels's credible and important research can, in light of the human capacity for direct *knowing,* become support for our breaking with belief altogether. And my so arguing does not diminish the great legacy of Pagels's work, which is its contribution to an absolutely new understanding of the formation of the Church. As I have found throughout my experience, we all stand on the shoulders of our ancestors, even as we evolve and find ways to supersede the progress they have fought hard to attain.

So, let's look at what Pagels has said about the Church's elevation of belief over the dissenting voices of the early centuries that followed the time of the historical Jesus.

# 9

# THE EARLY YEARS OF
# CHRISTIANITY
# ACCORDING TO PAGELS

## The Emergence of a New Community

ELAINE PAGELS'S WORK DEPICTS the early sects as inspired by stories of Jesus. They did not see themselves as Christians in the way we might identify ourselves as Christians now, but as Jews—and others—who revered Jesus as a great interpreter of God's law.[24] Their initial gathering places were not in churches as we think of them today. "From the beginning," Pagels says, "what attracted outsiders who walked into a gathering of Christians. . . was the presence of a group joined by spiritual power into an extended family."[25]

And what bound them together was perhaps more a communion of spirit, a new and different kind of community than had existed before—one that included Jews, Greeks, slaves, and the free.[26] Joining this new family also meant leaving their birth families because Rome persecuted both converts and their families. "In the eyes of their relatives," Pagels writes, "converts were joining a cult of criminals—a choice that could be suicidal for the convert, and disastrous for the family left behind."[27]

In contrast to prevailing practice for those who tended the ill, Christians took no money.[28]

> Members of the Christian "family" contributed money voluntarily to a common fund to support orphans abandoned in the streets and garbage dumps. Christian groups also brought food, medicines, and companionship to prisoners forced to work in mines, banished to prison islands, or held in jail. Some Christians even bought coffins and dug graves to bury the poor and criminals, whose corpses otherwise would lie unburied beyond the city walls.[29]

Stories drove the growing movement, and there was not a single body of beliefs that characterized those who participated. Pagels writes:

> What sustained many Christians, even more than belief, were stories—above all, shared stories of Jesus' birth and baptism, and his teachings, his death, and his resurrection. Furthermore, the astonishing discovery of the gnostic gospels—a cache of ancient secret gospels and other revelations attributed to Jesus and his disciples—has revealed a much wider range of Christian groups than we have even known before. Although later denounced by certain leaders as "heretics," many of these Christians saw themselves as not so much *believers* as *seekers,* people who "seek for God."[30]

## The Competition for Control

These stories were not transformed into the gospels of the Bible in the way that newspaper articles immediately follow the events of today, nor were they transformed into books within months or in the few years that it now takes modern books to appear. The New Testament Gospel of John—perhaps one of the most prominent factors in the later formation of the Church—may have been written a hundred years after Jesus's death.[31] What was particularly significant about the New Testament Gospel of John was that, among all of the books of the New Testament, it formed the foundation for the *content of the beliefs* that most specifically defined the price of membership into the much different community that the Catholic Church later offered. And yet, the Gospel of John was not necessarily representative of the stories that galvanized the early Christian movement. This goes directly to the heart of the story told by Pagels in *Beyond Belief* as she recounts her assessment of the significance of the discovery of the gnostic gospels:

As I worked with many other scholars to edit and annotate these Nag Hammadi texts, we found that this research gradually clarified—and complicated— our understanding of the origins of Christianity. For instead of discovering the purer, simpler "early Christianity" that many of us had been looking for, we found ourselves in the midst of a more diverse and complicated world than any of us could have imagined. For example, many scholars are now convinced that the New Testament Gospel of John, probably written at the end of the first century, emerged from an intense debate over who Jesus was—or is. To my surprise, having spent many months comparing the Gospel of John with the gnostic Gospel of Thomas which may have been written at about the same time, I have now come to see the John's gospel was written in the heat of controversy, to defend certain views of Jesus and to oppose others.[32]

Earlier, in *The Gnostic Gospels,* Pagels wrote:

> We now begin to see that what we call Christianity—and what we identify as Christian tradition—actually represents only a small selection of specific sources, chosen from among dozens of others. Who made that selection, and for what reasons?[33]

And later, in *Beyond Belief,* she wrote:

> I was amazed when I went back to the [New Testament] Gospel of John after reading [the gnostic Gospel of] Thomas, for Thomas and John clearly draw upon similar language and images, and both, apparently, begin with similar "secret teaching." But John takes this teaching to mean something so different from Thomas that I wondered whether John could have written his gospel to refute what Thomas teaches. For months I investigated this possibility, and explored the work of other scholars who also have compared these sources, and I was finally convinced that this is what happened.[34]

What made the New Testament Gospel of John unique among all other books of the New Testament and the gnostic gospels was its assertion that Jesus was God, that he was divine, and that his body was resurrected in physical form.[35] It is from John that the phrases that proclaim Jesus to be "God from God, Light from Light, true God from true God" come.[36] Pagels says, "Although John's formulations have virtually defined orthodox Christian doctrine for nearly two thousand years, they were not universally accepted in his own time."[37]

Of Thomas's view, she says, "The cluster of sayings I take

as the key to interpreting Thomas suggest instead that everyone, in creation, receives an innate capacity to know God."[38] John argued, says Pagels, that "humankind has no innate capacity to know God. What John's gospel does—and has succeeded ever after in persuading the majority of Christians to do—is claim that only by believing in Jesus can we find divine truth."[39] Yet, no one knows who wrote the Gospel of John.[40] But in John, the process of belief became primary and exclusive as a means to encounter God.

What an encounter with God meant was also in controversy. For Thomas, Pagels suggested, it meant an experiential and personal *identification* with God: "I am Thou." For the Jewish mystic Martin Buber, the encounter could not transcend an experiential *connection*: "I and Thou." But neither form of such direct encounter is allowed or encouraged by the Church.[41]

*The Secret Book of John*, one of the gnostic gospels, also says that human beings have an innate capacity to know God, suggesting, says Pagels, "that we have a latent capacity within our hearts and minds that links us to the divine—not in our ordinary state of mind but when this hidden capacity awakens."[42]

So, by the end of the first century, there were stories written not to convey history but to create a history that would create a new future for an emergent political-religious movement. In that way, the competition for ownership of the legacy of Jesus was on.

The debate over which stories represent the authentic version was not simply between those who were called gnostics and those who eventually defined the structure of the present Bible. Among the gnostics, there were plenty of disagreements as well. However, what the gnostics seemed to hold in common was their resorting to a process of personal experience in the form of personal revelation and visions as the means to authenticate the message. Speaking of the disagreement between the gnostic *Apocalypse of Peter* and the gnostic *Secret Book of James,* Pagels notes that the stories differ in identifying the apostle to whom Jesus imparted secret information, but that each has the same implication:

Each asserts the superiority of gnostic forms of secret tradition—and hence, of gnostic teachers—over that of the priests and bishops, who can offer only "common" tradition. Further, because earlier traditions, from this point of view, are at best incomplete, and at worst simply false, gnostic Christians continually drew upon their own spiritual experience—their own *gnosis*—to revise and transform them.[43]

And among the gnostics were those who disregarded the apostles altogether as a reliable source of information about Jesus, arguing that Jesus appeared not to the original Twelve, but to other disciples:

Gnostic authors often attribute their own traditions to persons who stand *outside* the circle of the Twelve—Paul, Mary Magdalene, and James. Some insist that the Twelve—including Peter—had not received *gnosis* when they first witnessed to Christ's resurrection. Another group of gnostics . . . say that the disciples, deluded by "a very great error," imagined that Christ had risen from the dead in bodily form. But the risen Christ appeared to "a few of these disciples, who he recognized were capable of understanding such great mysteries," and taught them to understand his resurrection in spiritual, not physical, terms.[44]

So the dispute in the second century came down to "who decides?" Pagels says:

Valentinus and his followers answered: Whoever comes into direct, personal contact with the "living One." They argued that only one's own experience offers the ultimate criterion of truth, taking precedence over all secondhand testimony and all tradition—even gnostic tradition! They celebrated every form of creative invention as evidence that a person has become spiritually alive. On this theory, the structure of authority can never be fixed into an institutional framework: it must remain spontaneous, charismatic, and open.

Those who rejected this theory argued that all future generations of Christians must trust the apostles' testimony—even more than their own experience. For, as Tertullian admitted, whoever judges in terms of ordinary historical experience would find the claim that man physically returned from the grave to be incredible. What can never be proven or verified in the present, Tertullian says, "must be believed, because it is absurd." Since the death of the apostles, believers must accept the word of the priests and bishops, who have claimed, from the second century, to be their only legitimate heirs.[45]

Among the gnostics, Valentinus was a prominent figure who articulated a view that was more difficult for the anti-gnostics to dispel. Valentinus did not dispute the need for a church around which the Christian movement might organize. What he disputed was the idea of apostolic authority. Rather, he would place authority in the achievement of a spiritual "maturity" achieved by the ability to make direct contact, as evidenced by visions:

> Valentinus claims that besides receiving the Christian tradition that all believers hold in common, he has received from Theudas, a disciple of Paul's, initiation into a secret doctrine of God. Paul himself taught this secret wisdom, he says, not to everyone, and not publicly, but only to a select few whom he considered to be spiritually mature. Valentinus offers, in turn, to initiate "those who are mature" into his wisdom, since not everyone is able to comprehend it.

> What this secret tradition reveals is that the one whom most Christians naively worship as creator, God, and Father is, in reality, only the image of the true God.
>
> ... Achieving *gnosis* involves coming to recognize the true source of divine power—namely, "the depth" of all being. Whoever has come to know that source simultaneously comes to know himself and discovers his spiritual origin: he has come to know his true Father and Mother.[46]

This maturity—what I would call *skill*—presented, of course, the greatest challenge to those who would build the church upon the authority of the apostles and the bishops who claimed to be descended from them.

Valentinus was also the author of a much more feminine view of the Divine than the bishops of the church that would ultimately prevail. Pagels writes:

> Valentinus, the teacher and poet, begins with the premise that God is essentially indescribable. But he suggests that the divine can be imagined as a dyad; consisting, in one part, of the Ineffable, the Depth, the Primal Father; and, in the other, of Grace, Silence, the Womb and "Mother of the All." Valentinus reasons that Silence is the appropriate complement of the Father, designating the former as feminine and the latter as masculine because of the grammatical gender of the Greek words. He goes on to describe how silence receives, as in a womb, the seed of the Ineffable Source; from this she brings forth all the emanations of divine being, ranged in harmonious pairs of masculine and feminine energies.[47]

The gnostic Gospel of Philip also suggested that the event of baptism is not the same for everyone. For some, it is an event marking the embrace of a belief, beyond which nothing really happens. For some, there is the experience of the mystery of the holy spirit. The difference, says Pagels, "involves not only the mysterious gift of divine grace but also the initiate's capacity for spiritual understanding."[48]

Whoever undergoes such transformation, says Pagels, quoting Philip, "no longer is a Christian, but a Christ."[49] By dividing converts into two groups—a common group and a group of elites—these gnostics created what Irenaeus saw as a problem for the Church. The elites were actually encouraged, Philip felt, to challenge scripture and thereby the faith of most believers.[50]

In short, whatever else gnosticism represented, it was a direct challenge to the authority of the bishops and priests of orthodox Christianity who would create an institutional approach based solely in belief and authority.[51] And, among the gnostic documents were specific techniques for achieving the spiritual maturity that represented the skill to connect directly, including turning attention inward, quieting the mind with meditation, chanting specific sounds, achieving ecstatic states, and activating the potential that is latent within all of us.[52] For these very reasons, Pagels suggests, gnosticism did not lend itself to creation of a mass religion:

> In this respect, it was no match for the highly effective system of organization of the catholic church, which expressed a unified religious perspective based on the New Testament canon, offered a creed requiring the initiate to confess only the simplest of essentials of faith, and celebrated rituals as simple and profound as baptism and the eucharist. . . . Without these elements, one can scarcely imagine how the Christian faith could have survived and attracted so many millions of adherents all over the world, throughout twenty centuries.[53]

# St. Irenaeus

Among those who opposed the gnostic view, there is no personality more prominent than Irenaeus, the orthodox bishop of Lyons in Gaul, present-day France. Irenaeus understood quite clearly that the views of Valentinus offered "nothing less than a theological justification for refusing to obey the bishops and priests," rendering their teachings no more than elementary doctrines, while the gnostics "claimed to offer more—the secret mysteries, the higher teachings."[54]

About 180 CE, Irenaeus struck out at the claim of "heretics" that "they possess more gospels than there really are," complaining that such writings had already won approval from Gaul through Rome, Greece, and Asia Minor.[55] At that time, Irenaeus wrote a five-volume text entitled *The Destruction and Overthrow of Falsely So-called Knowledge,* apparently referring to the later discovered gnostic gospels as blasphemy and heretical.[56] Pagels writes:

> Contemporary Christianity, diverse and complex as we find it, actually may show more unanimity than the Christian churches of the first and second centuries. For nearly all Christians since that time, Catholics, Protestants, or Orthodox, have shared three basic premises. First, they accept the canon of the New Testament; second, they confess the apostolic creed; and third, they affirm specific forms of church institution. But every one of these—the canon of Scripture, the creed, and the institutional structure—emerged in its present form only toward the end of the second century. Before that time, as Irenaeus and others attest, numerous gospels circulated among various Christian groups, ranging from those of the New Testament, Matthew, Mark, Luke, and John, to such writings as the *Gospel of Thomas,* the *Gospel of Philip,* and the

*Gospel of Truth,* as well as many other secret teachings, myths, and poems attributed to Jesus or his disciples. . . .

Yet by A.D. 200, the situation had changed. Christianity had become an institution headed by a three-rank hierarchy of bishops, priest, and deacon, who understood themselves to be the guardians of the only "true faith." The majority of churches, among which the church of Rome took a leading role, rejected all other viewpoints as heresy. Deploring the diversity of the earlier movement, Bishop Irenaeus and his followers insisted that there could be only one church, and outside of that church, he declared, "there is no salvation." Members of this church alone are orthodox (literally, "straight-thinking") Christians. And, he claimed, this church must be *catholic*—that is, universal.[57]

Interestingly, the views of Valentinus may have been more popular among the followers of Jesus during that time. Pagels writes:

We do not know how members of Irenaeus's own congregation reacted to his pleas [to condemn Valentinus and his followers], although we *do* know how distressed he was that the great majority of Christians initially accepted the Valentinians' view of themselves. . . . [Irenaeus] wrote that most Christians regarded them as among their most influential and advanced members. In his own time, Valentinus had been widely respected as a teacher by his fellow Christians in Rome.[58]

So the debate raged on.

# Constantine the Great

Elaine Pagels argues that it was not Irenaeus who won the debate that competed in forming the Catholic Church's ultimate perspective, but "the revolution initiated by the Roman emperor Constantine." In 312, Constantine converted. In a short period of time, he ordered amnesty for Christians. Nevertheless, Constantine "chose to recognize only those who belonged to what may have become, by his time, the best-organized and largest group, which he called the 'lawful and most holy catholic church.'"[59]

With this recognition came financial support. Constantine ordered property previously confiscated from Christian churches to be returned and compensation paid for damages. "Besides allocating money to repair damaged churches," Pagels writes, "Constantine ordered new ones to be built, including, tradition says, a magnificent church of St. Peter on the Vatican hill in Rome and the Church of the Holy Sepulcher in Jerusalem." He encouraged the bishops to ask for whatever funds they needed, and he made imperial food supplies available to the church to feed people in need.[60] At the same time, Constantine suppressed Jews, forbidding them to accept converts and threatening Jews who attempted to prevent other Jews from converting to Christianity with being burned alive.[61] Further, Pagels writes:

> During the transitional decades after 312, Constantine subjected the Roman empire to a massive restructuring and shifted the underpinnings of imperial power. What he did . . . was transfer the empire's basic allegiance from the . . . Gods of Rome, to the foreign God [Christ] worshiped by those whom his predecessors had persecuted for atheism.[62]

Constantine convened the council of bishops at Nicaea, from which emerged the Nicene Creed, which established "the list of twenty-seven writings which would become the New

Testament."[63] That creed "would become the official doctrine that all Christians henceforth must accept in order to participate in the only church recognized by the emperor—the 'catholic church.'"[64] At the same time, Constantine ordered the cessation of all heretical gatherings—those that were not part of this official movement of the new and most organized church.[65] Constantine died in 337.

And the repression of dissident writings followed:

> The discoveries at Nag Hammadi show how widespread was the attempt "to seek God"—not only among those who wrote such "secret writings" but among the many more who read, copied, and revered them, including the Egyptian monks who treasured them in their monastery library even two hundred years after Irenaeus had denounced them. But in 367 c.e., Athanasius, the zealous bishop of Alexandria—an admirer of Irenaeus—issued an Easter letter in which he demanded that the Egyptian monks destroy all such writings, except for those specifically listed as "acceptable," even "canonical"—a list that constitutes virtually all of our present "New Testament."[66]

Athanasius proclaimed that humankind was incapable of emulating Christ. "All that human beings can do—*must* do—is believe," says Pagels, in characterizing this position, "and receive the salvation that God alone can offer."[67] Pagels further says:

> What this revolution did accomplish was to enhance the authority of bishops identified as catholic and to establish their consensus, expressed through the statements of the creed, as defining the boundaries of the newly legitimate faith. To this day, someone who asks, "Are you a Christian?" is likely to follow with questions about propositional beliefs: "Do you believe that Jesus is the Son of God? Do you believe that Jesus Christ came down from heaven to save you from sin?"[68]

# St. Augustine

Even as early Christians were arguing over the question whether Jesus was Christ—that is, whether Jesus was divine—there was a common perception of the message of the Old Testament book of Genesis. In *Adam, Eve, and the Serpent,* Pagels writes:

> I came to see that for nearly the first four hundred years of our era, Christians regarded *freedom* as the primary message of Genesis 1-3—freedom in its many forms, including free will, freedom from demonic powers, freedom from social and sexual obligations, freedom from tyrannical government and from fate; and self-mastery as the source of such freedom. With Augustine . . . this message changed. In the late fourth century, Augustine was living in an entirely different Christian world . . . for Christianity was no longer a dissident sect. The Christian movement . . . [had come] into imperial favor. . . . Christian bishops, once targets for arrest, torture, and execution, now received tax exemptions, gifts from the imperial treasury, prestige, and even influence at court; their churches gained new wealth, power, and prominence. Christians, who once defiantly proclaimed their freedom against their persecutors, now found that their old rhetoric—and even their traditional understanding of human nature and its relation to social and political order—no longer applied to this new circumstance, which made them allies of the emperor. In a world in which Christians not only were free to follow their faith but were officially encouraged to do so, Augustine came to read the story of Adam and Eve very differently than had the majority of his Jewish and Christian predecessors. What they read for centuries as a story of human freedom became, in his hands, a story of human bondage.

Most Jews and Christians had agreed that God gave humankind in creation the gift of moral freedom, and that Adam's misuse of it brought death upon his progeny. But Augustine went further: Adam's sin not only caused our mortality but cost us our moral freedom, irreversibly corrupted our experience of sexuality (which Augustine tended to identify with original sin) and made us incapable of genuine political freedom.

. . .

Augustine's theory of original sin not only proved politically expedient . . . but also offered an analysis of human nature that became, for better and worse, the heritage of all subsequent generations of western Christians and the major influence on their psychological and political thinking.[69]

Sex and sin became synonymous, according to Augustine. Pagels writes:

Augustine believes that by defining spontaneous sexual desire as the proof and penalty of original sin he has succeeded in implicating the whole human race, except, of course, for Christ. Christ alone of all humankind, Augustine explains, was born without *libido*—being born, he believes, without the intervention of semen that transmits its effects. But the rest of humankind issues from a procreative process that, ever since Adam, has sprung wildly out of control marring the whole of human nature.

What, then can remedy human misery? . . . Augustine's whole theology of the fall depends upon his radical claim that no human power can effect such restoration. . . . Part of our nature stands in permanent revolt against the "law of the mind"—even among the philosophers, even among the baptized and the saints. And since, he insists, everyone, even the most advanced ascetic, confronts the same continual insurrection within, Augustine concludes that humankind has wholly lost its original capacity for self-government.

Augustine draws so drastic a picture of the effects of Adam's sin that he embraces human government, even when tyrannical, as the indispensable defense against the forces sin has unleashed in human nature. His analysis of internal conflict, indeed, leads directly into view of social conflict in general. *The war within us drives us into war with one another . . .* [and] *hence, two good men can be at war with one another* [emphasis added].[70]

Within the Catholic Church itself, Augustine's views were initially resisted. There were parties and factions within the Church. Augustine's response makes it absolutely plain why the belief process entwined with an authoritarian institution is so dangerous, as we can now see emerging in the American political realm in the midst of calls for a Christian government and nation. Pagels writes:

Augustine, too, became a public figure and ruler of a community. When his authority was challenged by the rival church of Donatists, Augustine came to appreciate—and manipulate—the advantages of his alliance with the repressive power of the state. . . . Donatist Christians denounced the "unholy alliance" between Catholic Christians [and] the Roman state . . . [insisting] that the church must employ only spiritual sanctions and not force.

Yet Augustine abandoned the policy of toleration. . . . [A]fter beginning with polemics and propaganda, [he] turned increasingly to force. First came laws denying civil rights to non-Catholic Christians; then the imposition of penalties, fines, eviction from public office; and, finally, denial of free discussion, exile of Donatist bishops, and the use of physical coercion. . . . Augustine came to find military force "indispensable" in suppressing the Donatists.

. . .

After Augustine had spent more than thirty years battling Donatists, he was dismayed to confront Christians he called the Pelagians who, despite many differences . . . shared with the Donatists . . . an insistence on free will. When his own party was outvoted in the Christian synods, Augustine unhesitatingly allied himself with imperial officials against the clergy who defended Pelagius. . . . By insisting that humanity, ravaged by sin, now lies helplessly in need of outside intervention, Augustine's theory could not only validate secular power but justify as well the imposition of church authority—by force, if necessary—as essential for human salvation.

. . . [F]ar beyond his lifetime, even for a millennium and a half, the influence of Augustine's teaching throughout western Christendom has surpassed that of any other church father.[71]

. . . Augustine insists that [Adam and Eve's] single, willful act permanently corrupted human nature as well as nature in general. . . . Augustine's position is paradoxical in that he attributes virtually unlimited power to the human will but confines that power to an irretrievable past—to a lost paradise. According to Augustine, human power alone reduced us to our present state, in which we have wholly lost that power. In our present state of moral corruption, what we need *spiritually* is divine grace, and what we need *practically* is external authority and guidance from both church and state.[72]

. . . [W]hat Augustine says, in simplest terms, is this: human beings cannot be trusted to govern

themselves, because our very nature—indeed, *all* of
nature—has become corrupt as the result of Adam's
sin. In the late fourth century and the fifth century,
Christianity was no longer a suspect and persecuted
movement; now it was the religion of emperors obli-
gated to govern a vast and diffuse population. Under
these circumstances, as we have seen, Augustine's
theory of human depravity—and, correspondingly, the
political means to control it—replaced the previous
ideology of human freedom.

. . . From the fifth century on, Augustine's pessimis-
tic views of sexuality, politics, and human nature would
become the dominant influence on western Christianity,
both Catholic and Protestant, and color all western
culture, Christian or not, ever since. Thus Adam, Eve,
and the serpent—our ancestral story—would continue,
often in some version of its Augustinian form, to affect
our lives to the present day.[73]

Constantine brought the government into alignment with the
needs of the Church, but Augustine brought the Church into alignment with the needs of the government. The process of belief was
what made this alignment possible.

The fundamentalist right in the United States would apparently like to see such a merger again today.

# IO

# A SPIRITUALITY WITHOUT BELIEF

## The Question We Need to Ask

ELAINE PAGELS, ALONG WITH OTHER scholars, opened a can of worms. Their work translating the so-called gnostic gospels is a grenade thrown into the chapel. It is the child's pronouncement that the king has no clothes. Pagels rather carefully and yet candidly offers a brief and personal observation on the implication of her work. Speaking of those whom the orthodox called heretics, she says:

> What such people seek, however, is often not a different "system of doctrines" so much as insights or intimations of the divine that validate themselves in experience—what we might call hints and glimpses offered by the luminous *epinoia*. . . . Engaging in such a process requires, of course, faith. The Greek term for *faith* is the same one often interpreted simply as *belief,* since faith often *includes* belief, but it involves much more: the trust that enables us to commit ourselves to what we hope and love. . . . The sociologist Peter

> Berger points out that everyone who participates
> in such tradition today chooses among elements of
> tradition.
>
>           . . .
>
> This act of choice—which the term *heresy* origi-
> nally meant—leads us back to the problem that ortho-
> doxy was invented to solve: How can we tell truth
> from lies? . . . Orthodoxy tends to distrust our capacity
> to make such discriminations and insists on making
> them for us. Given the notorious human capacity for
> self-deception, we can, to an extent, thank the church
> for this.[74]

There are several conclusions drawn by Pagels in these few
sentences. And all of them turn upon assumptions—assumptions possibly made due to a lack of the very experience that
represents what Valentinus called *gnosis* and I call *knowing.* I'll
address the assumptions that appear in Pagels's summary one at
a time.

First: *What such people seek, however, is often not a different
"system of doctrines" so much as insights or intimations of the
divine that validate themselves in experience—what we might call
hints and glimpses offered by the luminous* epinoia.

Here, Pagels does an implicit transposition that is apparent
only from the different perspective I have suggested in this book.
She places "insights or intimations of the divine" ahead of experience, by suggesting that experience validates the former. By
doing so, she suggests that insights and intimations—whatever
those might represent for her—are separate from experience,
rather than the first mental glimmerings that cognize an experience and represent the initial understandings that *follow* the direct
experience of the great mystery. If we give credit to the knowings that arise in the form of experience as separate and prior to
the rational understandings that our beautiful but limited brains
attempt to distill from raw experience, then the first apprehension
of the heart's knowings would always precede our insights and

intimations. They do not validate but inform our efforts to elaborate and communicate.

Second: *Engaging in such a process requires, of course, faith.*

There are a couple of big assumptions here. First, "such a process" must refer to a process of seeking. But, as we all know, seeking can rely on sharp tools or dull. We can seek by relying upon others or by relying upon ourselves. We can seek through belief. Or we can seek by honing our inherent capacity for knowing. "Seeking" is generic, not specific. It does not say how we can seek in a way that is calculated to find. It begs the question of how we might profitably seek. Second, there is an "of course" that assumes agreement in the reader. If one person of "faith" is speaking to another person of faith, then the "of course" might be assumed as given and justified. But I am not a person of faith. Yet, my story is deeply spiritual. I have sought and found. I have done so with neither belief nor faith. So what is meant by faith becomes the crux of Pagels's interpretation and the counterpoint to my own. Does seeking require faith? I have argued that not only is the answer no, but the belief which Pagels suggests to be an element of faith blocks our finding.

On that point, there is an illustrative vignette in one of Southwestern mystery writer Tony Hillerman's books—which one, I don't recall. In this particular story, Hillerman's protagonist Joe Leaphorn, a Navajo policeman, is investigating the scene of a murder with his FBI friend. Leaphorn is walking in expanding semi-circles from the railroad track near where the body was found. The agent asks Leaphorn what he is looking for. Leaphorn replies that he doesn't know. The agent asks what Leaphorn means by that. Leaphorn responds that, if he knew what he was looking for, he wouldn't find what he's not looking for.

If we are looking for the "divine," we won't find what is actually there. I'm also reminded of the story about the man who is looking for his lost keys under the streetlight. "Is this where you lost them?" his friend asks. "No," the man replies, "but the light is better here." We are habituated to looking for the divine in the light of belief and faith as it has been promulgated by religion.

Third: *The Greek term for* faith *is the same one often inter-preted simply as* belief, *since faith often* includes *belief, but it involves much more: the trust that enables us to commit ourselves to what we hope and love.*

I've addressed faith and belief on the terms Pagels has ascribed to them, but trust is another matter that is perhaps the fulcrum upon which so many people teeter. I hear about trust most often in the context of personal relationships, as in these questions: Can I trust this person I love to . . . (tell me the truth, do what they say, and so on)? Can I trust myself to make the right decision?

Trust is what we turn to when we don't know how to know. When we know, we can move with confidence that we are mov-ing in the right direction even if we don't know where it leads. Perhaps that is a way of speaking of faith, but it is a faith that depends not on belief. Pagels's syntax directly suggests that com-mitment depends upon trust, and that trust depends upon faith, which requires an element of belief. All of that is unnecessary if you know how to know. Pagels's analysis is just that: it is a men-tal formulation working outside the capability of the mental to find what can only be found in the heart's knowing. Faith seeks a knowing, but it is crippled by its dependence upon belief and betrayed by its reliance upon trust. If the seeking needs trust, it has not cultivated knowing.

Does faith bring us to an experience of the divine? In a way, Pagels answers her own question in the negative with the next statement.

Fourth: *The sociologist Peter Berger points out that everyone who participates in such tradition today chooses among elements of tradition. . . . This act of choice—which the term* heresy *originally meant—leads us back to the problem that orthodoxy was invented to solve: How can we tell truth from lies? . . . Orthodoxy tends to distrust our capacity to make such discriminations and insists on making them for us. Given the notorious human capacity for self-deception, we can, to an extent, thank the church for this.*

There is a tautology in Pagels's analysis here. One could argue that the human capacity for self-deception, if one were to accept her premise in that regard, is a consequence of—not a motivation for— the Church's adoption of the strategy of selling the process of belief as the exclusive means to find connection in one's life. The belief peddled by the Church is the spiritual equivalent of hospital life-support for an untreatable and terminal condition of human suffering, which is precisely the diagnosis the physician Church has given the human patient. It is the Church that has engineered what is perhaps the greatest deception perpetrated in human history, and it has sold that deception to the most vulnerable among us. And now we characterize the deceived as suffering from a "notorious . . . capacity for self-deception"?

Thank the Church? For making our moral choices for us? For the Church's calculated denial that humans can make real and competent moral choices without the intervention of a fabricated authority? This is a crime that is at least equivalent to the active participation of the Church in the colonization of indigenous peoples of the Americas, including the southwestern United States, where I live, and Peru, where I have visited. The crime is the propagation—from a pulpit of authority with a whip of condemnation—of the myth that humans are incapable of distinguishing truth from lies while the Church disingenuously prevents them access to the very means of making such distinctions. The Church burned the evidence of contrary theological opinion that would have revealed the lies. That alternative theology correctly identified skill—maturity—as the necessary condition for activating the capacity for knowing. By this elaborate falsehood that denies the heart's capacity for knowing, the Church has trapped Western humanity for more than a millennium in the mind of religion. Quite without the necessity of belief, faith, or trust, the heart has the capacity to know our inherent connection to all that exists, including that mystery—a mere taste of which confirms its benevolent relationship to our lives and our purpose for being. Atheism, in its equally ignorant denial of the skilled spiritual alternative to religion, is a naïve accomplice in an ongoing crime. Rather than deriving a genuine experience of connection from the Church's process, we have been left with generations of shame and guilt passed from priests to all the Church's children and a lot more of us as well.

In effect, Pagels argues, if one belief is found not to be credible but is part of a larger movement that provides the community of support for which we look to a spiritual process, perhaps it is best not to throw out the holy child with the holy water. Instead, she suggests, we should look within the religious traditions for more palatable beliefs. Her life's work is of immeasurable value. She has provided us with uncomfortable facts of extraordinary implication. But her final comments diminish their significance as she leaves herself within the faith tradition that inherently relies upon belief. She points us back to the tools used by the authoritarian hierarchy she has just eviscerated. Still, she has asked the right question: Can we touch the divine without a faith of trust and belief? It is one that we all need to ask and answer for ourselves.

My answer is that we can, through our own knowing, touch the mysteries that we call divine, or by the proverbial ten thousand names. Perhaps we can do so fully only *without* the belief that stands as our own projection. One could argue that the Church's imposition of a process of belief has itself enhanced the human capacity for self-deception. Our natural capacity for hope draws us to both beliefs and a faith that subjects us so easily to the deceptions that others would impose upon us when we are ignorant of the means by which we can connect directly. The projections of our own faith and belief block the very directness of the experience that we ultimately seek.

Pagels seems to suggest that some mix of faith, belief, hope, insight, and trust will get us there. My experience suggests that what gets us there is an inherent knowing that whispers to us even before we learn the skill of listening more deeply to its clear voice. Even the whisper—just one taste—is enough to propel and compel us. At our most fundamental level, we know we are connected. Yet, if our souls become distracted or remain in the weak posture that reflects a lack of skill development, we cannot amplify the underlying knowing of our connectedness into the deep relationship that is grounded in intention, imagination, and a self-identified soul in functional relationship with the body. The mind's design does not accommodate the experience of connection and can do no more than translate the experience into some understanding. The division of labor reflected by our various forms of intelligence has given *knowing* to the heart field as its gift and *connecting* as its means. The mind is not big enough to grasp the answer to the question that Pagels has posed to it. That is for the heart to do. And the heart is incapable of belief.

Is it my intention to denigrate seeking? Not at all. I simply want to promote finding and to do so with a process that acknowledges the human capacity for choice—the very capacity that the Church would call heresy and shame me for claiming. And I have Pagels, in part, to thank for clarifying the question. It was my reading of Pagels's work that helped me to understand that I had come to that amplified sense of connection quite without belief at all. Her work does not purport to fully examine the question she raises, and her work is not limited by the absence of that examination. But it does reach the difference between faith and knowing. It is in that distinction that we will find ourselves, our connection to the great mystery, and the means of making our own moral choices that underwrite the very purposes of our lives.

## The Experiential Alternative to Belief, Faith, and Trust

As I looked back on my own spiritual path, I found that the process upon which my exploration went forward did not depend on belief. Over time, I came to a rich and expansive experience of connection with all that exists without having to form beliefs that would become the objects and articles of faith. While my experiences would be followed by provisional understandings, my experience of connection came directly to my senses in the same measure and manner that I can sense an apple. I found a collaborative relationship with various aspects of what I will call the "mystery" called by the proverbial ten thousand names. During that time, I was able to discover how to know my soul's purpose and feel an internal ignition of a passion for the soul's work. I found a contentment that did not depend upon a fantasy of a continuing state of happiness, a life without significant challenges, or the denial of death itself. I, as soul, do not fear death, even as my body instinctively senses the danger that death defines. I feel I have already had a taste of the "afterlife." And my absence of fear arose from experiences that have nothing to do with the Church's promise of redemption for a soul imprisoned in a sinful body. I was able to transform my personality from a self-centered, projecting, energetically predatory hologram of a traumatized, fearful, and defensive body to an increasingly softer but fierce and independent partner for a soul trying to get some traction on a chaotic planet. I did so with a *process of personal experience.*

In retrospect, I was able to see that belief and personal experience are distinct *processes.* For me, it was not a matter of searching out some non-churchy version of Christian beliefs more palatable to a rational mind and consistent with the best scholarship. It was not a matter of finding the best set of ethical principles that a rational mind could muster. Nor was I searching for a set of beliefs completely distinct from Christian beliefs, such as those offered by the traditions of India, Persia, China, or Japan, or the set of beliefs currently being distilled from a postmodern engagement with indigenous shamanic traditions. I certainly looked at those. But what I found was simply that belief—as a process without regard for any particular content— was unnecessary.

Even at the beginning, belief was not a significant aspect of my spiritual path. Instead, I tasted and dabbled. In my twenties, I spent a couple of years with Transcendental Meditation that were very influential. I was asked to try a mantra and use it in combination with a daily practice. I didn't have to believe anything to do that. Curiosity was enough. Powerful experience arose from that practice.

By my mid-thirties, I started what would become several years of work with Native American–style sweat lodge practice. During that time, I layered on a stint with Swami Rama and practices based in yoga philosophy. I explored those practices without having to buy the philosophy, even as I found guidance and valuable experiences there. The next decade layered on numerous serious vision quests. That was followed by more than a decade studying indigenous healing traditions in Peru, including numerous encounters with the entheogenic plant medicines ayahuasca and huachuma.

During the decades of wandering these experiences consumed—parallel to my very conventional life in a thirty-year marriage with children while practicing law in a small community—my meditation practices continued and evolved. My marriage, children, and law practice each emerged as significant mirrors and teachers. Throughout this time, I enjoyed and suffered many extraordinary peak spiritual experiences. But I also remained suspicious of belief. It seemed the skepticism of my lawyer mind would rise to examine any particular meaning that might offer itself to explain my unusual experiences. I formed conclusions, understandings, theories, hypotheses, and sympathies for various ideas, but belief seemed neither necessary nor helpful.

That is not to say that I had not had some early experience with belief. By my late twenties, I had already gotten over the teenage rebellion that propelled me from my family's Methodist Church and the belief-based atheism that followed. I began to maintain a live-and-let-live approach to other people's beliefs—along the lines of "you can have your beliefs and I'll rely on my mind, thank you very much." It didn't matter if I thought your beliefs were just—well—*unbelievable*, so long as you didn't try to impose them on me. "Your beliefs are your beliefs," I thought, as I automatically conceded the entitlement of everyone to have them. My strongest beliefs during those first decades were atheistic, an experience that contributed to my emerging spiritual work primarily by its failure to address what was bubbling up from my heart.

As I moved beyond that immature and reactive embrace of atheism, I found myself experiencing a certain neutrality about churches and religions themselves. They were largely irrelevant to my day-to-day life. They didn't bother me, and I didn't bother them. That was my attitude until I read Pagels's *Adam, Eve, and the Serpent.*

Through Pagels's scholarship, I saw that the Catholic Church expressly adopted a process of belief as the foundation of its salvation theology while declaring a personal spiritual experience—a direct connection with God—as heresy. That was enough to get me to an understanding that belief is itself a process, one completely distinct from a process grounded in personal experience.

But there was quite another insight I received from reading Pagels's book. She recounted how Augustine's interpretation of the Genesis story, based in his personal struggle with sexuality, became central and enduring Christian dogma. It was Augustine who characterized humans as inevitably and irretrievably sinful, thereby condemning humans to a life of suffering with death as the final punishment. In other words, the early Church constructed a container made of the process of belief into which it poured the notion of Jesus's divinity. Augustine came along and filled that container with more beliefs until the cup ran over, leaving room for nothing else except perhaps the compassionate tincture of individual priests.

Reading Pagels's account, I realized my engagement of shamanic and mystical technologies of consciousness over many years had given me numerous direct encounters with the very archetypal elements found in the biblical story of Adam and Eve. I had seen and felt the garden, the serpent, and the masculine and feminine figures in it. I tasted the fruit, perhaps in more than one way. In ceremony literally held in the garden of the Amazonian jungle, I heard voices speaking and instructing me, directing my consciousness toward more skillful ways of engaging with the mystery from which I sensed the voices to have originated. In such a ceremony, I "gave birth" to a field of light I subsequently interpreted as my soul and watched as it entered my heart.

Over time, I experienced an energetic version of the universal archetype of the cross (which is distinct from the Christian crucifix) in the form of two "ignitions"—highly energetic bursts of energy felt in the center of my chest. The first had to do, in my early interpretive efforts at forming understandings, with a coming together of my own feminine and masculine natures in an event sometimes called the "inner marriage." That first ignition can be represented as the horizontal bar of a cross. On the heels of that ignition came a second made possible by the first, one that felt to me to be a joining of heaven and earth at the threshold of the human heart, forming the vertical member of a cross. "Heaven and earth" were for me not beliefs, but metaphorical ways of labeling mysteries beyond my understanding, though not beyond my ability to experience directly in some degree through my inherent capacity for knowing.

And, during a very modern psychodrama version of the ancient practice of shamanic journeying, the soul that arose centrally in my consciousness during prior experiences returned to its home in the "heaven" dimensions for the visit that is reported in a variety of ways by many who have had near-death experiences. During this other-dimensional sojourn, I encountered a love so unconditional and overwhelming that I have absolutely no doubt of the reality of such love as the common denominator of the cosmos, although that description is itself an interpretation of the mystery beyond the capacity of the mind, acting alone, to grasp. And, years later in a another jungle ceremony, I also encountered a similarly powerful but different quality of the same love emanating—in my mental interpretation of the images and thoughts that accompanied this experience—from the heart of the earth. That experience has repeated itself many times. Each time this has occurred, it has been serpents that ushered me there. The mere sight of them evokes deep joy.

What first became clear as I read Pagels's work was that I had encountered the elements of the Genesis vision in my own direct experience. I had no previous belief, Augustine's or otherwise, regarding the garden. Coming from personal experience, my interpretation was at a polar opposite to Augustine's interpretation that the Church had adopted as dogma for the regulation of belief. But another perspective emerged that was perhaps even more important. I began to see the belief process as inherently destructive to the unfolding of human potential.

As I read more deeply into Pagels's work and that of scholars working with the same material, I began to connect the dots. I began to see the role of Christian belief in propagating or tolerating widespread misogyny, violence, genocide, and exploitation of both humans and our earth. With that larger view, I became appalled, not only at the Church's historical role, but at my own ignorance. With that, my prior indifference to the Catholic Church and religion—and my earlier tolerance for belief in general—quickly faded. From there, it was easy to see the role that belief plays, quite beyond Christianity, among political, economic, and other religious movements in general. Christianity is not alone in marketing belief as a sufficient basis for justifying all manner of destructive and predatory human behaviors. Belief is the stock in trade of most religious fervor. It is also aggressively marketed by modern media, which was schooled in the propaganda movements that mobilized populations into world wars.

My reading broadened. I found relevant research pointing to a significant difference between brains of conservatives and liberals and between brains of males and females. Male brains, research now suggests, are biologically predisposed to higher levels of fear, sexuality, and violence than are female brains. Conservatives are predisposed to more fear and less flexibility when faced with change than are liberals. As I dug more deeply into research regarding the biology of belief—how conscious and unconscious beliefs affect the body as a whole—I began to see that *any* belief has a way of blocking an efficient and effective use of the variety of intelligences of the body. More specifically, I began to see how belief blocks the intuitive intelligence of the heart that is critical to the emergence of a passionate sense of soul purpose.

Seeing belief as a biological blocking agent sounded a bit like addiction. I found a connection in the emerging theory about addiction. Recent thought suggests that addiction arises not primarily from an unnatural chemical hijacking of cellular receptor sites but from a misplaced effort to experience connection. This new perspective suggests that, once connection is found or re-established, addiction ends far more easily. In other words, addiction has more to do with *why* we are engaging in a particular behavior than *what* the particular behavior is. A little more research revealed that others have already argued the connection between religious belief and addiction. When we use a process of belief to mimic the experience of connection we lack, it is little different in function than using alcohol, heroin, or other numbing agents to kill the pain of disconnection or to mimic a sense of connection. All of these addictive behaviors override the variety of intelligences that underwrite functional behavior and the achievement of human potential alike.

I was already aware of a growing body of research that supports the ancient notion that the heart itself is a powerful center of intelligence. Holding attention in the heart in a particular way not only supports positive health outcomes but allows for thinking that is less grounded in fear. That research provided a way of understanding how to find in the body the sense of connection that spirituality seeks. Before starting this book, I had practiced holding attention in my heart as a means of experiencing connection for more than ten years. With that personal experience, I could embrace an understanding that holding attention in the heart provided a sense of connection deep in the body that a mere mental belief cannot touch.

To be clear, I'm not talking about the negative effect of particular beliefs—although different beliefs can have different effects—but about the negative effect of the *process* of belief itself. Nor am I equating with belief the brain's linear processes that are belief's more sophisticated cousins, such as hypotheses, understandings, conclusions, logic, differentiation, comparison, rationality, analysis, critical thinking, and so on. All of these other processes are what we commonly lump into the notion of *thinking*. Thinking processes are the substance of higher-order mental operations, necessary to what we do yet not sufficient, acting alone, to enable us to reach our potentials. But those higher-order mental operations do not, and need not, include belief. Belief mimics thinking, just like heroin and religion can mimic connection or temporarily numb out the pain of its absence.

While we can trace the origin of particular beliefs to external sources, the process of belief cannot be understood without regard to the biology that makes it possible to entertain belief at all. Belief is possible only because there is something in brain and body structure that entertains belief as a thought form in the first place. When viewed in this way, it is possible to see that even positive beliefs have inherently negative consequences. If the brain is holding a thought formed of belief, there is far less motivation to engage the raw experience that might displace the belief-thought, particularly if the belief prohibits access to raw experience or suggests that personal experience is unnecessary. Declaring personal experience as heresy is religion's failsafe. If we believe we can't choose, we won't choose. Our belief in belief will keep us tethered, like the adult elephant that will remain tethered to the tiny stake from birth. And if we don't cross the yellow tape, we won't find out that the Church has lied to us.

If the brain is occupied with belief, the rational and holistic capacities of the brain *and* the intuitive capacities of the heart are blocked. Belief overrides our ability to *know* what raw experience suggests to a beginner's mind and to *envision* the big picture through which we are invited to navigate. In that way, all belief—positive or negative—is self-limiting. And, if your immediate reaction to that assertion is that a belief such as "I am unique, important, worthy, and capable" is not self-limiting, consider that the heart can *know and experience* your unique importance and capability far more effectively than a consciously held belief that is fighting against a body-based, traumatized subconscious that believes—in the body's own way of "believing"—exactly the opposite.

Belief, I concluded, blocks the very openness upon which evolutionary adaption and human survival depends, not to mention the realization of human creative potential. Of the range of possible mental activities, belief appears to be the most accessible, most primitive, most dangerous, least skillful, most unnecessary, lowest common denominator, and most subject to manipulation of all expressions of human intelligence. Belief is a parasite that distorts human intelligence. It is the enemy of that form of human intelligence that arises from direct, personal experience. Belief is the most common agent of dissociation, separating consciousness from the very body upon which consciousness depends to activate the intelligences that underwrite individual growth, creativity, and contentment. It blocks the door to the internal exploration from which insight arises and from which personal creativity emerges.

Of the various processes of our broader intelligence in operation—knowing, understanding, and visioning—belief alone is injected into consciousness from the outside without benefit of some legitimate validating process. Belief is held as a mental position complete and sufficient in itself, without regard for or aid from any direct, personal perception. As the Church instructs, we *have to accept its beliefs upon authority.* To belief, my inherent individuality is irrelevant, which is precisely why belief process is so dangerous. Belief allows someone who has no access to an experience of who they are to proclaim, "I believe, therefore I exist," and to join in common purpose with those who proclaim the same belief. And that community can function without the limitations of the inherent human morality that is sourced finally and solely from a conscious and coherent heart operating in collaboration with a brain that forms rational understandings grounded in vision and informed by experience.

Yet belief forms the foundation of much of our educational curricula, political process, religion, "non-religious" spirituality, and scientific and medical thinking. It is at the root of the cult of expertise that has overtaken common sense and dominates modern culture. Belief is the foundation of patriarchy. Religion did not, by any means, invent patriarchy, but it perfected it. Religion did so by expressly adopting belief *process* as its foundation and linking it with hierarchical authoritarian structures. Belief process and a primary human reliance on it are inherently dangerous—forming the very root of the planetary crisis that humans have manufactured. Limiting the use of the brain's processes to belief is like feeding the body with processed foods alone. That input will dominate human behaviors if not balanced with the other forms of human intelligence. We are living out the consequences of that domination now.

As an alternative to that rutted road, we can forge an entirely separate path. We can shape our spirituality around the process of personal experience grounded in a heart-based knowing that collaborates with brain-based understandings and visions. Such a spirituality finds in an honest scientific method a partner, not an enemy. To achieve this collaboration of intelligences requires skill development, the substance of which involves learning both how to control attention and where to put it. Research shows how holding attention in the heart can lead in that collaboration when a state of *heart coherence* is achieved. Belief has no role in that process and, to the contrary, can block it. Because belief is easier than skill development, we have to bring intention and will to changing our reliance on it.

# II

# A DEFINING DIFFERENCE
# BETWEEN
# RELIGION AND SPIRITUALITY

## *Two Distinct Processes*

SURVEYS ARE TELLING US there are big shifts in how people are relating to religion. Yet over-simplistic survey categories that offer "religious," "spiritual but not religious," and "none" as the only options cover over a complexity that has not been fully explored. Both the current surveys of changes in religious identification and the debate over what those changes mean are overlooking an apparently subtle but critical point.

While there are many contrasts that might be identified in the attempt to sort religion from spirituality, I doubt any is more important than the difference between the respective processes of belief and personal experience. Those two processes define all other differences, including the distinct ways in which we experience connection, treat the body, form community, discover a sense of belonging, define sacred space, create relationship, define psychological understandings, engage with ritual, pray, relate to the earth, make war, make love, express love, receive love, create identity, address fear, approach death, engage the death transition, find passion and purpose in our lives, engage with the mystery we sometimes call God, and engage the different forms of human intelligence. These two processes form distinct ways of addressing the big questions humans face: Who am I? What is my purpose? How do I answer the first two questions? What is the purpose of life in general? How can I find the community upon which my survival depends? How can I feel safe, find connection, and overcome the persistent feeling that I am alone and helpless?

The surveys and debate have focused on the *content* of religious beliefs, as though *what* we believe, rather than the fact *that* we believe at all, is the central issue. Atheists and the religious believe with the same fervor. They just believe differently. The debate has not focused on the question of whether belief is in and of itself what defines religious engagement. Nor have we defined the difference between religion and spirituality other than in terms of the content of belief. We have not focused upon the difference between a perspective based in belief, on the one hand, and a perspective based in personal experience without belief, on the other.

In *Beyond Belief,* Pagels proposed a way of looking at the divide that did not make the distinction between a process based in belief and one that is not. She characterized the difference between the orthodox and the gnostics, respectively, as *believers* and *seekers.*[75] She revealed her personal disinclination to embrace in their entirety the *content* of the beliefs mandated by the orthodox Church even as she found comfort in the *community* she discovered in a particular modern Catholic congregation. Her own research had caused her to identify less with the content of traditional beliefs and more with a process of *seeking* in the hope and faith that we can *find*. In her conclusion to *The Gnostic Gospels* and throughout her later writing, she elucidated the tension between the "authority of one's own experience and that claimed for the Scriptures, the ritual, and the clergy."[76] Indeed, a central point of her subsequent book, *Beyond Belief,* was to contrast the early diversity of the Christian movement that offered the possibility of a personal connection with God with the Catholic Church's eventual prescription of beliefs that denied the possibility of such an experience.

What I saw in this distinction between believing and seeking was something different yet. Pagels did not describe the difference between competing beliefs as different processes, as such. I saw a direct competition between processes. My merely assigning the word "process" to the distinction is little different than the contrast she described. However, what is different is my perception that personal experience is a process with more than a single dimension. There is the personal experience of *seeking,* and there is the personal experience of *finding.* The latter, I would suggest, is a function of skill—what the gnostic Valentinus possibly meant by *maturity.*

Pagels's analysis of the gnostic gospels—particularly in her description of the teachings of Valentinus—suggested that personal experience had two tiers, the latter of which was called "maturity." The notions of skill and maturity both suggest a developmental process, but skill seems a bit more hard-edged and clear to me. And, in my own experience, skill development has been central in a way that the notion of maturity simply doesn't describe.

Pagels suggests that the difference between the gnostics and the orthodox results in two kinds of experience.[77] She is clear that the gnostic approach involves a very intense and solitary interior journey.[78] The gnostic could not accept on faith what others said, except as a provisional measure, until one found one's own path. Pagels writes:

> As the gnostic teacher Heracleon says, "people at first are led to believe in the Savior through others," but when they become mature "they no longer rely on human testimony," but discover instead their own immediate relationship with "the truth itself." . . . Only on the basis of immediate experience could one create the poems, vision accounts, myths, and hymns that

gnostics prized as proof that one actually has attained *gnosis.*[79]

Pagels also suggested that gnostics saw creativity to arise from the visionary capacity of one who had cultivated one's own gnosis:

> Like circles of artists today, gnostics considered original creative invention to be the mark of anyone who becomes spiritually alive. Each one, like students of a painter or writer, expected to express his own perceptions by revising and transforming what he was taught. Whoever merely repeated his teacher's works was considered immature.[80]

Orthodox Christianity, on the other hand, articulated a different kind of experience. Pagels further writes:

> Orthodox Christians were concerned—far more than gnostics—with their relationship with other people. . . .[81]
> . . . The orthodox church gradually developed rituals to sanction major events of biological existence: the sharing of food, in the eucharist; sexuality, in marriage; childbirth, in baptism; sickness, in anointment; and death, in funerals. The social arrangements that these events celebrated, in communities, in the family, and in social life, all bore, for the orthodox believer, vitally important ethical responsibilities. . . . Even their pagan critics noticed that Christians appealed to the destitute by alleviating two of their major anxieties: Christians provided food for the poor, and they buried the dead.[82]

In others words, the orthodox Church saw in community the formula to casting a larger net. Whatever else the Church has become, it still provides the most accessible opportunity for spiritual *community*. And it has done so by embracing the process of belief, thereby creating a very low hurdle for entry, while the gnostics set the bar high, requiring an ultimate skill as the price of initiation for "communing." What a church teaches, Pagels quotes Origen as saying, "must be simple, unanimous, accessible to all."[83]

The defining element of Christian faith, says Pagels, is *belief* in the resurrection of Jesus in the *physical* body, as first seen by Peter.

> If the New Testament accounts could support a range of interpretations, why did orthodox Christians in the second century insist on a literal view of resurrection and reject all others as heretical? I suggest we cannot answer this question adequately as long as we consider the doctrine only in terms of its religious content. But when we examine its practical effect on the Christian movement, we can see, paradoxically, that the doctrine of bodily resurrection also serves an essential *political* function: it legitimizes the authority of the certain men who claim to exercise exclusive leadership over the churches as the successors of the apostle Peter. From the second century, the doctrine has served to validate the apostolic succession of bishops, the basis of papal authority to this day.[84]
>
> . . . Whatever we think of the historicity of the orthodox account, we can admire its ingenuity. . . . First, as the German scholar Karl Holl has pointed out, it restricts the circle of leadership to a small bank of persons whose members stand in a position of incontestable authority. Second, it suggests that only the apostles had the right to ordain future leaders as their successors. . . . What the apostles experienced and attested their successors cannot verify for themselves; instead, they must only believe, protect, and hand down to future generations the apostles' testimony.[85]

In other words, something that can only exist as a matter of belief, that is not susceptible of rational proof or direct personal experience, became the basis of the church's distinct doctrine *as a matter of strategy.*

Contrast this to the view of gnostic Christians, who saw the resurrection not as a "unique event in the past" but as a symbol of "how Christ's presence could be experienced in the present" in the form of spiritual vision.[86] Such visions were not dismissed by gnostics as fantasies or hallucinations but were seen as "spiritual intuition. . . into the nature of reality."[87] Clearly, having direct experience and accepting exclusive apostolic authority were two different ways of being Christian, two processes that could not co-exist.

And, among the gnostic views, was a notion of the *evolution* of a Christian:

> . . . One of Valentinus' students, the gnostic teacher Heracleon (c. 160), says that "at first, people believe because of the testimony of the others . . ." but then "they come to believe from the truth itself." So his own teacher, Valentinus, claimed to have first learned Paul's secret teaching; then he experienced a vision which became the source of his own *gnosis* .[88]

But, asks Pagels, is that personal vision reliable?

> But how are visions received, and which are divinely inspired? Practically speaking, who is to judge?. . . Although most of the people at that time—Jews, pagans, and Christians alike—assumed that the divine reveals itself in dreams, many people then, as now, recognized that dreams may also express only wishes and hopes, and that some may lead to fatal delusions.[89]

It is an important question. And the answer is precisely what divides those who live in and rely upon a process of belief from those who are able to attain what the gnostic Valentinus called spiritual "maturity."

Any of us who have had a significant inner experience have also had to confront two challenges. First, we have to ask whether a vision is *real*, for that value of "real" which holds that the experience represents an actual encounter with other-dimensional intelligences. Second, there is the challenge of translating that experience into an understanding by which we can effectively, if at all, relate the quality and significance of the experience to other people, or even to ourselves. When we attempt to communicate such matters, we quickly come to realize that language does not work to transfer the full significance of experience. As the Asian traditions instruct, the finger that points to the moon is not the moon. Language is only indicative. It cannot replicate experience. What language can do is conceptualize what we have come to call "meaning" or "understanding." Meaning and understanding represent the interpretation of experience that is necessary for experience to guide our work in the world. Experience must be integrated into understandings that support meaningful action that is also guided by the visionings that map the way forward toward possibility.

The answer to Pagels's question is that we can ultimately know only for ourselves whether our own experience is real and whether the meaning we draw from it is helpful to us. How do you know when you connect with the mystery that we sometimes call the Divine? You'll know, just as I knew that a fish had taken my line. You'll know as you know you love your child. If there is doubt, you probably haven't connected. When you connect solidly, there is no doubt, even if understanding is difficult to come by. That knowing is entirely different from the belief that reaches even to an intensity of faith, which is the very hope and desire for connection that has not yet occurred.

If spirituality is indeed to be a separate process than religion, then we find that difference in, on the one hand, a religion that has a simple means of entry, a unanimous belief, and a door that is open to all who do not question the beliefs and, on the other hand, a spirituality based in an interior search fostered by the evolution of a sufficient skill to take that search from seeking to finding.

If you would propose to know and *be* the soul, experience is your only path. And breaking with belief is the only way to find your way to the raw experience that is the source of knowing. You can choose a faith community of believers and have a community of minds that foster mutual support. Or you can choose to commune directly with all that exists. On that path lies the community of the heart and the purpose of the soul. That latter community, which embraces the creativity of a unique individuality without a profession of common belief, is a community far greater in its expanse. But it does not offer the common community of humans in a culture dominated by belief. One may have to choose between the two. If we are to find the heart of spirituality, it seems that it is necessary to transcend the mind of religion. In doing so, we embark upon a more solitary—and paradoxically more connected—path.

## The Evolution Toward Maturity

In the early development of our intelligence, we are invited, often swayed, by culture to use beliefs to define our experience. Only as time and experience bring us toward a greater maturity do we use experience to define understandings that, even if not accurate, are more than mere beliefs unrelated to personal experience. Experience process is belief process turned inside out. As Valentinus suggested, we may turn our senses outward, whether toward belief or experience, before we are capable of learning the value and skill of turning them inward. Mind gathers information, whether we call that information facts, understandings, or beliefs, but the heart distills the direct knowing of experience into the higher-level understandings we have called *wisdom*.

Before we are capable of turning our attention inward toward the inner landscape in which personal experience is distilled into understandings, we must literally travel through developmental physiological stages. Our minds are capable of belief long before we are able to mature our skills of attention to the ability to encounter the heart as the source of direct knowing. Brain and heart operate on distinctly different intelligence programs. Each field of intelligence operates by a distinct process that forms a container for the particular quality of information that it processes. It is important to distinguish container from content, but it is also valuable to remember Marshall McLuhan's injunction. Like the medium is the message, so can the maturity of the container define the quality of its content.

Religious belief speaks to a level of human evolution in which the fearful and unskilled brain-mind predominates. Science also speaks almost solely to and about the brain-mind. The soul that represents our individual consciousness must emerge from its sleepy enmeshment with the undeveloped body/mind/personality in order to focus and abide adjacent to the heart if knowing is to take its rightful place as the observer/operator of the body's trilogy of intelligences. With the self-identified and focused soul seated in the heart portal, the soul can direct the orchestra of the analytic brain, the visionary brain-mind, and the connective heart in a harmonic expression of the soul's gift in purposeful work on the planet. Soul is the consciousness that operates behind and illuminates each of the body's distinct forms of intelligence, and it can do so effectively only when the soul is itself focused—which we experience as focused *attention*—the primary means of activating soul potential and a collaboration of human intelligences.

That harmony of intelligences is the potential of a spirituality grounded in personal experience—a spirituality supported by a skill of consciousness that is not innate, but learned. That harmony represents the marriage of mind and heart. It transcends a humanistic ethics limited to the brain-mind's analytic and rational processes by the discovery of an irrational and purely personal, heart-based morality. It facilitates the marriage of science's observation of the material world with the soul's internal heart knowing of all else, and it represents one aspect of the mythic and archetypal marriage of the masculine and feminine.

Perhaps, because we have not better understood the distinctions that the common terms "religion" and "spirituality" attempt but fail to define, we have not clearly identified the methods by which this harmony of human intelligences can arise. Among these, the development of a skillful internal attention and an open-ended exploration of the places we can put that attention are central. Asian meditation tradition has offered technologies that help us develop a skillful internal attention. Indigenous tradition not only offers us technologies and perspectives that avail an open-ended variety of places and dimensions we can place that attention, but also helps us to associate that attention with an experience we can call *soul* and with a living earth. These indigenous technologies of consciousness include what are now called *entheogenic* (generating the divine within) plants—plants that have the capacity to reveal soul and encourage it to emerge from its enmeshment with the unconscious body and become an agent of healing for the body and the earth. The opportunity to fuse meditation and indigenous technologies calls us to engage our personal capacity for a heart-based knowing—bringing our attention and souls back to our bodies and to our connection with the earth. There lies purpose.

# 12

# BELIEF'S EMPIRE AND THE ABSENCE OF EMPATHY

## *An Empire Built on Belief*

IF THERE IS AN INHERENT tension between the respective processes of belief and personal experience, then it should also show up in arenas apart from the religious and spiritual. Turning our attention toward American social and political culture, it is obvious that the same tension exists there. Our most powerful cultural players manage belief to achieve their goals, from the consumer industry to politics to finance to education. Simplistic perspectives are easier to manage than complex perspectives, and belief process provides a fabulous vehicle for the former. As I write, Donald Trump—a master manipulator of emotionally charged, simplistic beliefs—seems to be pushing the outer limits of using belief on his quest to capture the presidency. Early in his campaign, a Bible held in his raised hand revealed a form of that manipulation—the intersect between religion and politics—that is far older than Augustine. All of this is obvious. What is not so obvious is whether there is a way to change it. But it certainly cannot change without a pretty good understanding of how it works.

One approach to an understanding is to observe the parallel between what is occurring in the United States now and what occurred during the early evolution of Christianity. A quick look at the formula that underwrote the Catholic Church's longevity reveals these elements: the embrace of the process of belief and rejection of the process of personal experience; the creation of an exclusive community based entirely upon the process of belief; the adoption of particular beliefs that define the community; the creation of a source of authority to validate both the underlying process of belief and the particular content of the beliefs; governmental support and funding; a means of spreading the word; exploitation of women and suppression of their voices; and, lastly, beliefs that speak to the lowest common denominator of human emotion—fear—assuring the largest possible market for its message.

Once the Church convinced people to believe in belief, to believe in the inherent sinfulness of humanity, and that belief in the divinity of Jesus was a sufficient pathway to a salvation that redeemed them from sin, it had won the battle. When people believe that belief is a sufficient means both to address their inherent fear of death and provide a sense of community, almost any belief will do. And once people embrace belief as a means to address their discomfort, they are unable to hear the quiet, inner voice that provides the alternative to belief—that inner knowing from which the soul creates a pathway through suffering and fear to its unique destiny.

Among the present-day players using the Church's time-tested formula are Movement Conservatism, neoconservatism, neoliberalism, rich folks like the Koch brothers, the NRA, the Tea Party, the Republican Party, the Democratic Party, Wall Street, global corporations, climate change deniers, Ayn Rand individualists, libertarians, and a profoundly invasive technological media owned by just a handful of very wealthy individuals. How this strategy has warmed up and played out over the last century can be found in *Manufacturing Consent: The Political Economy of the Mass Media,* by Edward S. Herman and Noam Chomsky, where the authors argue that the mass communication media of the United States "are effective and powerful ideological institutions that carry out a system-supportive propaganda function, by reliance on market forces, internalized assumptions, and self-censorship, and without overt coercion" by means of the propaganda model of communication.[90] Propaganda relies, first, on the pre-extant and pervasive belief in belief and, second, on control of its content as the means of manipulating the behaviors of a public whose ability to see beyond that manipulation is fairly limited. Just like the Church.

Using a process of belief, both political parties have strategically divided voters into special interest groups that reflect particular beliefs, unencumbered by any understanding of the true complexity of managing a nation, leaving simplistic thinkers with the fantasy that they can participate meaningfully by voicing any narrow belief. And, in a way that is not commonly observed, the division of voters into single-issue interest groups paralleled another troublesome development over the same period: the emergence of specialization as a dominant force across all fields of cultural endeavor. Specialization has undercut not only the idea that competent citizenship depends upon the acquisition of a broad-based liberal education, but the idea that individuals are themselves competent to regulate their own lives without "research-based" direction by specialists. And the absence of an effective liberal education has made it far easier to make people dependent upon beliefs marketed directly to a neurology already addicted to the technological methods of delivery that now form the pipeline of belief.

For example, a "pro-life" position supported by a political party and a political church can easily delude simplistic thinkers into believing that their position should override any and all other social concerns. Because belief causes blindness, such thinking overlooks how the political party that has purchased loyalty with that position wages war on life in general with a shock-and-awe military campaign elsewhere in the world—never mind how many fetuses, babies, and children die in that process. The same pro-life belief similarly ignores how a party's economic policy has resulted in the poverty and malnourishment of not only fetuses, but babies, children, teens, and adults. Belief clogs thinking in such a way that inconsistent facts cannot get traction on the neurological pathways.

On the progressive left, one finds concern for rationality, research-based science, religious tolerance, tolerance in general, inclusivity, civility, peace, social safety nets, compassion, sustainability, and equal justice and opportunity in the areas of race, gender, education, and employment. Yet, even on the left, the embrace of scientific process has spilled over into common beliefs that only scientific method or rigorous scholarship can provide direction and that personal experience is not only unreliable, but prone to fantasy in matters of spirit and otherwise. And on the neoliberal left, no less than on the right, there is a persistent belief that more war will solve our Middle Eastern challenges, just as we persist in our War on Drugs despite overwhelming evidence of its failure. Belief is driving these positions, not a rational analysis of facts.

Armed with the belief that there is no God, and standing on the ground of materialist scientism, there are new belief-based priests who vehemently attack the beliefs of religion and religion itself. These include ideologues such as Daniel Dennett, Richard Dawkins, Victor Stenger, Christopher Hitchens, and Sam Harris. While Christianity's bad acts over the centuries make it an easy mark for criticism, these authors make the unscientific error of asserting that absence of proof is proof of absence (of evidence that there is a transcendent intelligence in the universe). Their atheism is no more than belief-process-based religion flipped upside down.

In the religion of science itself can be found some strongly held beliefs. Among them are the notion of genetic determinism, which assumes that genes are more powerful than environmental influences; the belief that evolution, in general, including human evolution, is based solely upon random genetic mutation that leads to selective adaptation over long periods of time; and the idea that the body is essentially a machine that can be modified simply by technological and pharmaceutical interventions—to name a few. The notion of genetic predetermination related to disease formation and pathological behaviors is the modern equivalent of the Church's Augustinian notion that we are born irretrievably burdened with a sinful nature that condemns us to suffering. The high priests of genetic science similarly promise a salvation from the condemnation of a genetic accident of birth. Patents are involved, which echo the exclusivity and funding of Catholicism as the state religion of Rome.

As a culture, we enshrine beliefs in the possibility and necessity of unending economic growth, American exceptionalism, and the strange notion that a vastly superior military can reshape the world for the better—"better" meaning that America can continue to maintain a higher standard of living than any other country while remaining "secure." The true believers embrace the specious notion that free market capitalism is the foundation of democracy, espoused by cynical and subsidized corporations that peddle that belief along with an infinite supply of other consumables. Some of us believe we are a democracy, and some of us believe we are an empire, and some believe that the two are consistent and beneficial. Simple to believe, but not true.

With a belief-process-based conservatism on one side, scientism on the other, and a corporate/capitalistic-leaning neoliberalism in between, the context and players have shifted since the Church embraced belief process, but the underlying competition of processes has not. Proponents of an internal, skilled process of embodied knowing, including those that would ally with an honest science, are denigrated or sidelined by all of these political groups, just as dissenters were pushed aside by the early Catholic Church as it achieved political cover and financial support from Rome.

When the Catholic Church prevailed more than 1,500 years ago, it did so, first, by capturing the market brand and message of a charismatic religious zealot. Second, it embraced a process of belief. Third, it partnered with the empirical political power of the day. That formula comes close to describing presidential politics of the present day.

Today, the competition is on to capture the market brand of the original American revolution and its experiment in constitutional democracy. Christian belief and the belief process itself remain a central part of political strategy as each side seeks to gain control of the modern American empire. America's corporate elites capitalize on the process of belief through control of the media and a good part of what are marketed as scientific studies. Both political parties and the corporate elite peddle the belief that America remains a democracy, since the legitimacy of their actions depend on capturing the support of those who still vote and discouraging or preventing the rest from doing so.

The political establishment of the left is more aligned with legitimate science but is also dominated by corporate capitalism, largely leaving voters to choose candidates already vetted by corporations. The personal experience that is the source of knowings that inform understandings has no voice or advocates in the political process. It seems that the only questions left in our political process are how fast and to what degree the corporations will be turned completely loose and how, not whether, we will wage a foreign policy based in overwhelming military superiority. As the purely financial self-interest of a governing elite pursues empire, Rome is burning once more. Despite our beautiful technologies, dark ages loom again. Without a belief in belief as a legitimate source of truth, this would be less likely to happen.

I would suggest that the central takeaway from this brief allusion to politics is that politics, like religion, is a mirror of the nature of human intelligence and that we have so limited our use of human intelligence by a belief process that even rational voices, in the presence of such pervasive belief, cannot save us from ourselves. There are scholarly, rational dissenters. Why are their voices not influential at the highest levels of power?

## An Absence of Empathy

Soldier-scholar Andrew Bacevich recently published *America's War for the Greater Middle East: A Military History.*[91] I picked up the book after reading an interview of Bacevich by Patrick L. Smith, Salon's foreign affairs columnist.[92] Bacevich, professor emeritus at Boston University, describes in his book the complete failure of America's foreign policy in the Middle East, with a detailed analysis of each military campaign or intervention over a period of thirty years.

In the conclusion of his book, Bacevich seemed to be playing directly to my antipathy regarding belief. Following his litany of the individual failures of America's interventionist policy, Bacevich says: "Through it all, a succession of American leaders—Republican and Democratic, conservative and liberal, calculating and naïve—has persisted in the belief that the determined exercise of U.S. military power will somehow put things right. None have seen their hopes fulfilled."[93]

Asking why we can't get out, he also asks, "How can it be that even today, large segments of the policy elite entertain fantasies of salvaging victory if only a smart president will make the requisite smart moves?" Answering his own question about the "persistence of these illusions," he identifies four "assumptions." Assumptions, of course, are equivalent to what I have defined as beliefs. The first assumption/belief is that Americans will prevail in what they see to be the "epic competition between rival versions of modernity—liberalism vs. fascism vs. communism." The second assumption/belief is that Americans are wise enough to "control or direct" the forces of this historical narrative and that the American way of life is inherently superior. The third assumption/belief is that America's superior military power "serves as an irreplaceable facilitator or catalyst in moving history forward toward its foreordained destination." The last assumption/belief is that the Islamic world "will embrace American norms." "None of these assumptions," says Bacevich, "has any empirical basis. Each of the four drips with hubris."[94]

Bacevich goes on to list four reasons that Americans don't make a serious challenge to the policies that arise from these beliefs. He cites the lack of any antiwar political movement or party, the tendency for "aspiring" politicians to "support the troops" (and therefore the war), the great profits that accrue to the military-industrial complex, and, finally, his view that Americans are "oblivious to what is occurring" and "take it as a given that U.S. policy will perpetuate the position of disparity that they consider their due."[95] Bacevich is correct, and belief is all over this American mindset.

Still, what really caught my attention was Bacevich's comment about *empathy* in the Salon interview:

> Right now I'm reading, in a manuscript, a book by David Hendrickson that's a critique of U.S. foreign policy. He's a political scientist who teaches at Colorado College and author of a number of other important books. He's one of these guys, I don't understand why he's not a household name. Brilliant work and certainly respected in academic circles, but he's not on "NewsHour" every night. One of many interesting points that he makes in his new book is the remarkable lack of empathy on the part of American policymakers. Not sympathy. Not deference. But an inability to see a situation as it appears to people on the other side.[96]

Bacevich is saying that American policymakers lack the ability to empathize. Let those two words settle in: *inability* and *empathy*. I thought Bacevich's mention of empathy put its finger on a glaring feature of Americans' attitude toward non-Americans. We are literally unable to put ourselves in the shoes of what are now millions of men, women, and children killed, maimed, or rendered homeless due to America's military actions in what Bacevich calls the Greater Middle East. There are at least hundreds of thousands of children—perhaps millions now—in this category that we commonly refer to as "collateral damage." Such "numbers" alone boggle the human mind. We literally cannot imagine what those numbers represent. We can see one dead immigrant child held in the arms of a Greek rescuer, but we cannot imagine, much less feel, the many. The heart has a greater capacity to do so than the mind—its reach is so much greater—but we have to acquire the ability to use it, and that inability seems so apparent now as the numbers grow so large. It seems ironic that our media reach is so much greater, able to transmit images around the world, but our human reach is so small.

One sees statements of sympathy—possibly grounded in an ability to empathize—from the religious (although we often get the opposite). Bacevich seemed intrigued and supportive to see the question raised by Hendrickson in the political realm. It is surprising to someone like Bacevich, perhaps, because it is obvious that actual empathy for the scale of human destruction wrought by the United States is completely incompatible with our self-justifying beliefs, while our occasional acknowledgments of battlefield "errors" are simply hypocritical and ludicrously transparent.

I emailed David Hendrickson at Colorado College to inquire about his treatment of empathy in his analysis of American foreign policy. Hendrickson generously replied with a copy of his manuscript and this comment: "There is a section in chapter two on 'The Golden Rule' that speaks most directly to the empathy question. I don't actually use that term, but Bacevich is right that the need for it—that is, the need to understand conflict as it appears to people on the other side—is indeed basic to my approach. I derive that precept from within the western political and religious tradition."[97] His eloquently simple statement of that precept is the Golden Rule: *Do unto others as you would have them do unto you.* He traces the historical preeminence of that rule in a review of prominent philosophers. Bacevich argues from facts; he is saying that what we have done simply hasn't accomplished what we intended. Hendrickson argues from the collective, preceptual wisdom of human philosophy; he is making the value judgment that philosophers make, suggesting that a simple rule of human behavior would be a better guide for our foreign policy.

I read Hendrickson's manuscript, a beautifully constructed resort to the roots of international law that illustrates how radical America's militaristic and imperialistic foreign policy is in comparison to the entire course of human history. Hendrickson and Bacevich are excellent scholars who are on the same page. And their voices, I suspect, cry out from the political and social wilderness of American foreign policy.

In further conversation with Hendrickson, he made it clear that both empathy and reason are necessary, that empathy and reason do not stand in opposition. I agree. Yet, the tool of scholarship is reason, and its resort is, as Hendrickson suggests, the various traditions that have expressed it time after time in the past. Scholarship explicates primarily from reason. By contrast, speaking from the spiritual side of the polarity formed by reason and empathy, I argue that it is only through the direct connection of the heart-field that a pure empathy can arise, and only then can empathy be rendered into a greater personal understanding by the abstraction of it through the reason, which is the tool of our brain/mind.

In our personal correspondence, Hendrickson asks the critical question that underlies our conversation: "Given the known partiality of human beings in how they distribute their empathy, is there a rule, or set of rules, that makes for a peaceful mode of living together?"[98]

My response is that his question begs another. Can a set of rules override the "partiality of human beings" that is itself the attenuation of the deep connection that gives rise to empathy in the first place? My answer to Hendrickson's question is no. Unless there is a capacity for the direct experience of connection that gives rise to empathy that can then be expressed rationally— as Hendrickson has done with the Golden Rule—I would say that the rule does not overcome the absence of its felt source. The rule presumes the ability to empathize. In addition to our rational scholarship, we also need to be talking about how humans touch that source and become empathetic. Reason appeals to the traditional rule of law based in the law of nature. The approach cannot be naysaid. But it can be ignored, which is the response of those humans who have no ability to empathize because they cannot bring their attention to the field of intelligence that we have long called "heart." What has gotten in the way of that is a long cultural tolerance of the process of belief and a scientific bias against the knowing of the heart while culture enthrones the reason of the mind.

What does this have to do with my book about belief and spirituality? In the context of my discourse on the deleterious effect of belief on a true spirituality, there is a point that the scholarly debate illustrates. We can and need to resort to traditional philosophic views that draw on precepts suggesting rules of conduct. Philosophy, of course, though sometimes sourced in *knowing,* is not *knowing* as I have defined it in this book, but the construction of rational understandings. It deals with values, reason, and language. It arises from the critical thinking that Bacevich and Hendrickson embody. But it does not reach to the *experience*—the *knowing*—of how another person is experiencing his or her life, or even how we experience our own. Reading Hendrickson and Bacevich, I have little doubt that both experience empathy and that empathy informs their work, but they are arguing from facts and reason. This is not a basis for criticism of their work. What is missing, however, is an identification of what is truly missing in the scholarly milieu in general. The American heart and soul have gone missing. There is little notice of their absence. With them has gone true empathy.

The alternative to the emphasis of scholarship is to define empathy *both* in its preceptual way, as the resort to philosophy requires, and in a perceptual way, as honoring our heart-field of intelligence requires. It is possible for one human to experience directly the state of being of another. This direct experience is a perception—a percept. While I see a preceptual emphasis as consistent with the rules of scholarly exposition, that emphasis can easily omit recognition of direct experience as the ultimate source of the understanding/precept that expresses wisdom—the kinds of wisdom that have resonated with people of good character over the centuries. Hendrickson and Bacevich are such people. Something in them *knows* that American policy is wrong and failing, and they resort to rational analysis and philosophy to develop a persuasive argument demonstrating what they know. But, to have that direct experience of another, one has to *connect* rather than merely think, analyze, or philosophize. The heart's knowing transcends the separation that thought necessitates and arrives directly at the experience that gives rise to what we need to acknowledge now as *un*common sense, having let go of our common sense in order to embrace our beliefs. When we have the experience of connection, when your child is my child—when I feel directly the pain of your child being killed in the same way I feel the direct pain of my own child's death—then we can no longer hold on to the fantasies, illusions, and conceits that we have enshrined in belief with all of the authority of a constitutional right accorded to religious freedom. Belief is the antithesis of direct and raw experience. Am I really free to believe what I want to believe, when doing so illustrates more than anything else the depth of human ignorance and accelerates the demise of human existence on the planet? I'm afraid the answer is probably *yes,* quite without regard to law and due to the mere fact that humans remain in a primitive state of evolution. But it does not make it wise to do so. Can humans design their own demise, using both reason and belief to do so? Yes, even if it is foolish. The free will that underwrites creation must allow for the prospect of failure. We are seeing the face of that failure now.

In a similar way, the open-ended nature of a world intelligently designed for evolutionary creation and creativity depends upon individuality reaching toward its unique expression. Individuality, however, without the foundational support of the field of heart collaborating with soul, becomes fertile ground for the development of the kind of "me-ness" that is the pathology of America's exclusive embrace of mind and disconnection from the field of heart intelligence. America has certainly lost touch with both heart and soul. The use of life and liberty to pursue happiness, for a person with soul and heart connected to the brain, is about a depth of creative purpose and expression—not the spreading out into broader shallows of entertainment, stimulation, and recreation. We do not need re-creation, but the novelty of creation that arises from a collaboration of mind, heart, and soul—a creativity that supports community instead of isolating the individuals from it. Creation without empathy is moving us—ironically—toward a dangerous form of *artificial* intelligence, artificial because it lacks the uniquely human, heart-based insight that allows us to serve each other in community. Instead, our analytic intelligence serves the increasingly technological exploitation of each other, addicting us to the technology itself while separating us further from each other. We are trying to fly on one wing. Analytic intelligence without heart intelligence is just another form of artificial intelligence; both are "AI," and both portend the same risks to humanity.

In the final analysis, empathy as a precept—compared to empathy as a percept—is as margarine to butter. The former remains merely an abstraction of the latter and behaves quite differently in our bodies. My partner, Darlene, is an *empath.* Through her, I have met many people—both men and women— who have the ability to *feel* others. For most of these people, it is a curse; they are continuously overwhelmed by the sheer volume and negativity of the information with which they are flooded merely by entering a space occupied by many people, such as a shopping mall. If they can control this quality of their nature by limiting the volume of information that comes in, then the empathy is a gift that can serve to help others. If they cannot, their empathy becomes a pathologic condition, just as the total lack of empathy at a cultural level is pathologic, as in the case of those powerful people who define our foreign policy. Indeed, we are overwhelmed by the bad news of the world and have shut our eyes and ears to it, particularly to that part we ourselves are causing. What is lacking in general is the *ability*—the skill—to be empathetic when we need to be, when that information is relevant. And it is always relevant when our actions begin to affect the lives of others and the condition of our planet. That skill is not a mental skill, but a heart skill. We cannot find it in precepts, but only in percepts—in the direct experience of the world and our companions on it through the capacity of skilled hearts to connect.

I agree with the *thinking* of both Bacevich and Hendrickson, without reservation or qualification. But even that high-quality thinking does not reach the kind of empathy that is part of a *knowing* that war cannot succeed. From that knowing, we can begin to develop the arguments of fact and reason. This knowing is not first and foremost a rational conclusion, although it is eventually so in collaboration with the rational resources of the mind. At its primary level, however, it is the knowing of wrongness, not as a moral conclusion, but as the whole-body apprehension that war and violence interrupt the very connection upon which human survival depends. Something in the design of humans and our planetary universe requires us to collaborate, communicate, and cooperate in order to survive. Empathy—the whole-body response to the experience of connection—is the first message from our bodies to our minds that we need to understand this fundamental, built-in imperative of humans: together we survive; together we move forward. Pre-rational infants know this fundamental rule before they can mentally apprehend it. Force and control do not and cannot ultimately serve this end. Of course, we may defend ourselves and our own, as Hendrickson acknowledges, but the irrational logic that morphs the Golden Rule into a pre-emptive *do unto others first and harder* takes us to the continual conflict that cuts across the very means of our survival. Add in technology, and we simply destroy ourselves more quickly, dripping blood *and* hubris. That is the current state of the world. Without the heart, there is only fear. With fear, there is only the logic of aggression. With fear, we cannot quit the kind of war that America now takes for granted in its idiotic illusion of being exceptional. Shifting perspective—a rare thought in itself—we might ask who now would even want to empathize with us? More and more, there are fewer who will.

My humble suggestion that humans as a whole would do well to dispense with belief is not accompanied by a shred of personal anticipation it will happen on a scale sufficient to shift public policy. Pandora's box was opened when we dropped the bomb on Japan. Rather than empathizing with the human cost of that decision and closing the box in the face of the horror America wrought then, we've jumped into that box to see how many more war toys were left, and we've increased the magnitude of bombing beyond Japan many times over with nothing positive having come from it.

We must, if I were to enjoin an action, *get out* of our rational minds long enough to discover the higher intelligence that resides in our hearts. We cannot fully either inform or express the potential preceptual wisdoms of our minds in the rational language of critical thinking without our having used our heart intelligence to empathize through direct connection with the planet and each other. I have zero confidence that our runaway-train political process can yield now to such a suggestion.

But *you* might. I am not writing to the body politic. I am writing for individuals who already sense that connection is the pathway to discovering their purpose and provides a possible pathway forward on the planet for the small communities that learn to hold hands with the earth and each other.

## The Teaching of Trees

By suggesting a necessary polarity and reciprocal relationship between precepts and percepts, I do not mean to suggest that knowing and reason are equal in importance. Knowing is primary, and reason follows. Empathy is not the handmaiden of philosophy's work. It is not mere eye candy on the arm of reason's political ascendancy, nor sentiment that softens reason's hard edge. It is not the little sister of science.

Reason has its season. In the great tree of human intelligence, reason and vision are the fruits of the tree, not the great tree itself. With its roots connected into the earth and its leaves touching the light of the sun, the essence of the tree is *knowing.*

Consider the great rhythm of trees' genius. In the abiding connection of tree to earth and sun, there is a breathing in. Sap rises up from earth to greet the inflow of sun's magic light. In this in-breath there is a joining together in the intimate darkness, the synthesis of photons—a marriage of light and matter, of heaven and earth. And there follows a breathing out as blossoms give way to fruit before sap flows rootward as the sun moves lower on our view of the equatorial horizon for the winter. The connection of the in-breath must precede the expression of the out-breath. The great rising up must precede the great return. The temporary fruits delight and nurture us for an all-too-short, sweet taste before change's cool winter renders them stale, even as the tree's underlying connection abides quietly but actively in the darkness of earth's chest. The connection of the great tree and the great rhythm of its breath—these are the source of its sweet gift that we have long taken in hand, preserved in glass jars, and handed around in church basements.

Wise reason and clear vision are blossoms and fruits of our own genius. But we have moved past the time of growing our own fruit in soil we know—soil in which we ourselves are rooted. Now our fruit comes with bar-coded labels from places unknown. You just don't know where it's been, but you might consider that it's not yours. Yes, we want the wisdom of reason emerging in its time from the maturity of the great tree of knowing, but we have moved too far from our own roots, and the preserved traditions are not enough to guide our pathways on a rapidly changing earth. We must rely again on our own knowings, our own roots. The human heart roots into the earth, drawing up the sap of life force to meet the frequencies of heaven's design born on the soul's light, breathing those forces out through the body and into creation. And we might well pray that politicians and priests alike quit tolerating the clearcutting of our forests to paper us with more mere belief.

PART FOUR

# HOW TO WORK IT:
# A TR(ILOGY OF) ACTION =
# TRACTION

# INTRODUCTION TO
# PART FOUR

PARTS ONE THROUGH THREE ARE no more than a necessary, if laborious, preface to Part Four. Without that explanation, it would be difficult to achieve my ultimate goal for this book, which is to describe a process by which we can identify directly with the soul, allow the soul to take the lead in healing the body, and discover soul purpose by using the sensuality of a body made available by that healing.

Part One described *what's at work* (soul, body, and heart); Part Two described *how they work* (a collaboration of the intelligences of knowing, thinking, and visioning operating from coherence); Part Three described *what resists it* (belief); and Part Four describes *how to work it*. The last part is simple enough. And, as I've said earlier, while the process is simple, it's not so easy to do.

There are some fundamental techniques necessary to progress in this process. They are intention, imagination, and focus of attention. There are entire books devoted to these techniques, so I will be brief. Belief is not required.

# Intention

All spiritual work leads with intention. Intention is a mental formulation of purpose. Intention guides the subject of thoughts, the trajectory of imagination, the focusing of attention, and how we place our attention.

# Imagination

Imagination gets a bad rap in American culture. Religion in particular doesn't want you to go there. Many scientists treat imagination as make-believe, although Albert Einstein felt it to be more important than what we could know or understand at any moment. Joseph Chilton Pearce wrote that "imagination is the capacity to create an internal image not present to the outer senses, which can then be used to enliven some particular potential waiting around in limbo for expression."[99] Pearce called this relationship a "strange loop," which is, I think, the same as what I have called coherent resonance.

There is a rich literature that treasures and elaborates upon the value of imagination. For my purpose, I will define imagination as the way in which the soul navigates the world. Through the heart portal, the soul uses the body's capacity for thinking and visioning in a way that it can project outward into the possible. We cannot lift an arm without first imagining it. Imagining a trip to the moon preceded forming an intention to get there, which is followed by imagining how to do it. Intention dances with imagination. What would I like to do? Let me imagine it. Then I can intend it and imagine how.

When we image-make, we create a subtle form of reality. The body experiences this as real. When we fantasize, we are creating an image to which the body responds, whether the fantasy is fearful or pleasurable. Imagination provides the subtle, organizing field by which our coherent hearts can reach out to resonate with coherent fields that, together with our own action, define what is possible in a particular moment of the world.

There is a continuum of reality from subtle to material. In this continuum, imagination is on the subtle end. Imagination is the beginning and pathway along that continuum. We use imagination to create the pattern that possibility represents, then follow the pattern to materialize a more substantial reality. Imagination, from this perspective, is real for that value of "real" that is relatively ephemeral. We can't create the new realities that represent the potential of the more substantial end of the reality continuum without it.

## *Attention*

The soul is made of consciousness, from which we derive awareness. Attention is the pointed focus of that conscious awareness made possible by the distillation of consciousness in the form of a soul, which has no earthly relevance without a body with which it can work. The collaboration of the body of matter and the soul of consciousness forms up the human. Self-consciousness, an extraordinary thing in itself, is how the soul experiences and knows itself as distinct from the body. Attention is what travels with intention by means of imagination. Meditation is a general technique that encompasses many techniques for learning how to focus attention as a function of intention and skill. Extreme sports and other dangerous activities tend to force us to pay attention, which is why we are drawn to them when we have not learned to develop the skill of focus with simple intention and practice. How much further and faster we can travel when skilled attention explores the cosmos through our three intelligences!

*\*\*\**

The process that brings us to the soul's skillful engagement of experience, which is the subject of this Part Four, has three steps. In Chapter Thirteen, I will focus on the primary step, which is to develop the strength of the soul while shifting identity to the soul itself. Chapter Fourteen will describe the task of healing the body, why that is important, and how the soul undertakes the task of healing the body. Soul does so by placing itself in the heart portal, enveloping the body, connecting itself to the fields of heaven and earth, and, finally, developing a working relationship with the body. In Chapter Fifteen I will talk about the role and value of the entheogenic plant medicines in these processes. Chapter Sixteen will focus on how the soul uses the body's sensuality to feel into purpose—to find those possibilities within which purpose lies.

# 13

# SHIFTING
# IDENTITY TO THE SOUL

ONE CENTRAL MESSAGE OF THIS book, if not *the* central message, is this: if you want to find purpose in your life and expedite the healing necessary to do that, you would do well to shift identity from the body/mind/personality to the soul. This is an experiential engagement. Belief will not work. Discovery of purpose requires you to achieve the coherence that brings traction to the process of translating soul gifts into planetary purpose. A self-identified soul is necessary for that to happen. This shift of identity is not a common process. It is not drawn from ancient tradition, nor is it a re-translation of tradition. I suspect that many people do this in a rather natural way without thinking about it. My own work seems to have opened a veil and allowed an insight into the potential of using this intentional process. My background of experience has allowed some insight into how a fusion of distinct wisdom traditions at this time in human history is making way for and necessitating a new process in the evolution of human consciousness. There are probably others teaching such a process, but I am not aware of them. It is, I humbly suggest, the next threshold in the evolution of human consciousness, one that is specifically intended to further the human enterprise of collaborative co-creation with the planet rather than provide the escape route from it.

This process does not replace healing, but provides the skill to make our efforts at healing ourselves more effective. Claiming the soul identity is the single most important step you can take if you want to make your subsequent efforts at healing effective. Effective healing, in turn, is the step that precedes the steps that lead to finding purpose. Claiming soul identity creates the platform upon which you can stand to guide your own healing. Healing creates a sufficient sensory platform from which the body can work with the soul to find purpose. That is the sequence.

Nor does this process replace the work of consciousness that aims toward "enlightenment." I suggest instead that what we have called enlightenment is a way station on the ultimate journey to the soul's creative engagement with the planet.

In this chapter, I'll describe how I begin to walk clients through this preliminary process. In my work with clients, I have to start with a construct—the description of the soul perspective. Then we proceed to acquiring a taste of the experience of being the soul. I tell my clients that the emphasis is not on healing, but on learning the skill of attention that is associated with shifting identity to the soul. Healing opportunities and events often arise during our work together. Moving soul into the heart portal, even for a taste, evokes real experience. When that happens, we may take advantage of such opportunities, but that is not our goal in this preliminary stage of work. Instead, we are after a preliminary understanding of the process and a sufficient experience of it to provide a basis for the daily practice that leads—with intention, commitment, and effort—to the skill that prepares the client for the more intense engagement of healing. Indeed, a primary reason that so many efforts at healing do not take or reach deeply enough is that the client does not have the attention skill that a shift to soul identity represents to integrate even powerful healing opportunities. Others cannot do the healing for us. We ultimately have to do it for ourselves, using the opportunities and interventions others provide for us. This is how we prepare ourselves to do that.

## *How a Session Looks*

There are two parts to each session. Sessions always begin with some conversation. They always end with a roughly equal time on the massage table.

Whether it is the first time or a subsequent coaching session, I ask questions to elicit how the client is looking at whatever challenge the client is dealing with at the moment. By understanding the client's view of the challenges and their response to them, I can see how they view themselves and their position in the world. Everyone has a way of looking at the challenges in their life. Everyone has a way of seeing how they fit in the world. I want to know how they deal with those questions. As the conversation proceeds, I notice how the client may be able to shift perspective on some questions but not on others. For example, we may learn how forgiveness of the perceived wrongs of another serves us with respect to a particular person in our lives but be quite unable to extend forgiveness to another person. Shifting fundamental perceptions is a process that invites cognitive dissonance, and the preliminary conversations serve to let me know how the client is walking into that inevitable ambiguity.

Once I have learned the client's way of seeing the world, I try to shift my language to meet the client's language as much as possible. Using my client's pre-existing frames of reference allows me to explain the construct of the soul perspective in a way that is most likely to allow them to receive it. I ask, for example, whether they have any belief or understanding about souls. If so, I ask them how they experience the soul. Similarly, I look for events in the client's experiences in which they have experienced a direct knowing. I identify that experience as such and label it for them so that they have a frame of reference for recognizing raw experience as distinct from belief or understandings.

I also use the preliminary conversation to explain the second part of the session that happens on the massage table. This part is about getting that experiential taste of the soul's presence in the heart portal. I explain that, although healings occur and insights arise during these table sessions, those outcomes are, frankly, not my primary purpose. I clarify that the purpose of the work is to learn a process that leads to the development of a skill. We are working together, I explain, to help clients learn how to take responsibility for their own healing. Then, before we start that piece of the work that occurs on the table, I explain in detail how it will work so that clients will have an expectation about what is going to happen once they have lain down and closed their eyes. This expectation will help clients relax with what is to follow, and it also prevents them from having to think as much during the table session as might occur if they were having to process the instructions while trying to relax. This preliminary review allows clients to clarify and ask questions before we start.

In this second part, we use imagination to make an image of the soul in order to elicit *the experience of being the soul.* I suggest an image for them and name that image as the soul. Then we work with that image in and around the body to establish the beginnings of a new relationship between the soul and body. If the client has had the good fortune at some time in their lives of having had the kind of peak experience that allows them to realize that they *are* the soul, we can work with the images associated with that experience.

The client lies on the massage table fully clothed, without shoes. Unless it is very warm in the room, I will typically offer the client a blanket. The blanket will help the body remain warm and comfortable during the process, but it also lends a certain womblike quality to the experience, helping the client's body to feel held. I assume a position in a chair at the client's head, ask permission to place my hands under the client's head, and use a cranial/sacral occipital technique that allows me to palpate the cerebral spinal fluid. The technique allows me to monitor the client's cerebral spinal fluid pulse, which provides me real-time, ongoing information about how the client is responding for the thirty to sixty minutes that the client may be on the table. The technique also tends to relax the client.

I often do this same process with a client by phone. In that circumstance, I ask the client to lie down with the phone positioned so we can hear each other. The process is essentially the same, with the exception that I cannot touch the client or monitor visual cues. However, I am able to monitor the pulse even without physical contact. I don't understand that, but my provisional understanding is inclined toward the idea that, when the client enters into this relationship with me, our fields connect, allowing me to experience the client's field directly.

Once I have connected with the pulse, I'll instruct the client in a breathing technique that will also help to relax the body. HeartMath's research has identified a breathing pattern that is optimal for relaxing the body and creating coherence.

The italicized words that follow are illustrative of the words I speak softly into the client's ear to guide the client's engagement with the process. Each client is different, and the approach requires flexibility. I do not memorize this guidance, but visualize a pathway which I describe as I accompany and lead the client. This approach leaves me entirely free to modify the approach as circumstances might require, since the client's experience to some degree defines the pathway. To be clear, this is illustration, not formula.

So the client hears me speaking softly in his or her ear in this way:

*Close your eyes and begin with the breath. Breathe deeply, slowly, gently, and silently. By deeply, I mean that you should breathe abdominally.*

Prior to the table session, I have explained that such breathing allows the diaphragm to drop to make room for the lower lobes of the lungs to fill fully. As the diaphragm lowers, it pushes the organs downward, causing the belly to rise.

*Breathe in and out through your nose unless the nose is blocked. By slowly, I mean that you should breathe several seconds in, with an optimal length of five seconds, but making the exhalation the same length—whatever the length of the inhalation—as the inhalation, without pause between the inhalation and the exhalation.*

Prior to the table session, I have explained that this breathing process is also one that must be learned with practice. A breath of such length that does not require effort is seldom accomplished without practice over time. And I re-emphasize this notion in the next instruction.

*By gently, I mean that, despite the goal of making a breath five seconds in length, you should not push yourself to breathe more deeply than is comfortable in the moment of your exercise. In any moment, on any particular day, there is an optimal length of your breath—one that is as deep as possible without pushing yourself to discomfort. There is a sweet spot, so to say, in the breath of the moment that is gentle to the body, without grasping, without effort, without any sense of having failed to make the most of your breath.*

*By silently, I mean that you should listen to the breath as it passes through your nostrils. If you can hear the breath and your nose is unobstructed, slow the breath until you cannot hear its sound, so that there is no sense of pushing beyond what the body will naturally accommodate in a relaxed, but intentional and focused state. Notice how the body relaxes just a bit as you slow the breath.*

*Breathe in this way for a few moments to establish your rhythm and allow the body to relax in the breath.*

Then I wait for a minute or two, watching the client's abdomen to see that a deep breathing pattern has started and monitoring the cerebral spinal pulse to see if the body is indeed relaxing in response to the breath. If it is, I affirm to the client that I sense the body to be relaxing and ask whether that is the client's experience. If it is not, then I take more time with the client to work with the breath.

> *Now, using intention and imagination alone, call to your attention. Call to it from wherever it has gone today, yesterday, and this past week. Call to it from wherever it has gone last month, last year, and, indeed, this lifetime.*
>
> *Because intention and imagination work instantly, you can see your attention arriving immediately in response to your call. See it forming as a sphere of light, just in front of your chest. Notice that the sphere of light is gently rotating, radiating its brilliant light and growing rapidly in intensity. And, because intention and imagination work instantly, know that your attention has fully arrived.*
>
> *Now, using intention and imagination alone, move this brilliant sphere of light into the center of your chest, which is the center of your heart portal as well. Know that this sphere of light is who you are and that you are the soul.*

Now the soul is situated in the center of the client's chest and the center of the heart portal. We have, for the moment, called to attention that has lodged itself in a variety of places throughout the client's life. The "lodging" of attention is a kind of memory. There are two kinds of such memory. One is the conscious memory that we associate with storage that occurs, as we understand it, in the brain. This memory has a visual or linguistic quality to it, or both. When we remember someone's name, we may remember the face as well, or just one or the other.

The second kind of memory is the memory held by the body, which is unconsciously held at a level from which it is not so easily called up. The body holds a memory of trauma in this way. It is more of a knowing, but a knowing held below the surface of consciousness and not fully integrated into conscious brain memory. Our common experience is that such memory is triggered by external events that bring either the memory or a reaction to the original traumatizing event to the surface. In this exercise, we are calling to the unintegrated awareness that the body has of this historic trauma because that awareness is a fragment of the soul. Calling it a fragment of the soul is both accurate and metaphoric. Attention is the expression of the soul's presence. Soul/attention becomes dispersed over the territory of the body and anywhere else awareness has gone out of the body. We experience the dispersal of attention consciously as distraction, a feeling that we are missing something of ourselves. We feel that something is not complete, and that is an accurate sense.

So, in this exercise, for just a moment, we are calling the attention from wherever it has lodged as an unconscious or conscious memory and asking it to reveal itself in the highly concentrated form of a self-aware, present soul. Despite this exercise, it is likely that the attention will disperse again, returning to its position before we called it. But we consider the possibility that our having called it to a point of focus and named it as the soul to which we have shifted our identity changes something very fundamental: "I am that soul positioning itself in the center of the heart portal located in the center of the chest of this body." It is a beginning. I continue, speaking softly to the client:

> *Seeing yourself in this moment to be the infinite being that is the nature of a soul, now seated in the heart portal in the center of the body, allow your light to project through the portal into the body. Make this projection ever so gentle, knowing the body to be its own being separate from the soul. Approach the body with respect and softness. Make your approach an invitation to the body to open, if it is so inclined, to receive your light. Know your light to be the light of which the entire cosmos is made, a light we know and*

*experience as unconditional love. This unconditional love is what you offer the body. And it is, indeed, what you are.*

Before the table session, I will often use the metaphor of a polarity defined by notions of the masculine and feminine to explain the relationship between soul and body. I suggest to the client to consider that the soul is the masculine in this relationship between soul and body. Soul is the field that penetrates the field of the body, the feminine aspect of the polarity, which receives the soul if it is so inclined. The body, as an entity distinct from the soul, experiences itself as distinct from the soul in its own unconscious way, even though body awareness is part and parcel of soul awareness. Because it is a distinct entity, the body experiences the new intensity of a focused soul as a separate entity proposing to enter. If the body's historical experience is one of trauma—as is the case for most of us in one degree or another—then the body will have formed a defensive posture relative to prospective intruders. In such a case, the focus of the soul may be experienced as a potential threat by the body. This is the basis of dissociation. Hence, the gentle approach by the self-identified, focused soul in this first iteration of an exercise that will be repeated time and again until the body feels safe enough to allow the soul to enter fully. I continue:

*Proceed without presumption that the body will receive you. Just as the male must await the invitation of the female before it approaches even with love and gentleness, so you now approach the body with love and gentleness, with respect and without the presumption of expectation. Your inherent connection with the body may cause the body to open, but you must await the body's signal that you may approach. And as the signal is received, nevertheless proceed slowly and gently as this new relationship is in its early stages of conscious formation. In your imagination, you can see that the body does open, in some measure that does not need to be quantified. Because there is a naturally strong connection between soul and its body even before a complete relationship can be established between soul and its body, there is openness. The body's openness to its soul allows you, as soul, to flow into that openness.*

*As the soul, imagine that your light expands and flows throughout the body, from the top of the head to the tips of the toes, to the tips of the fingers.*

*As you expand your light in the body, invite each and every cell of the body to open and receive your light. Make this invitation with respect, without presumption, and without the projection of any expectation that the cells will open to your presence. Extend your invitation for the cells to open in their own time and in their way, within the abiding presence of the unconditional love that is the felt nature of your presence in the body.*

*During this time, remain focused in the heart portal in the center of the chest. The soul, so to say, does not move. Rather, the soul radiates its light from its now fixed position in the center of the chest.*

This notion that the soul itself does not move is central to the process of the soul relating to the body and to all the benefits that flow from that relationship. While soul might be said to be making an appearance on the threshold of the time-space dimension, soul is not of that dimension. It is, rather, more of a visitor. It operates as a quantum field. In the metaphoric understandings of which our minds are capable, the soul "radiates." But it might otherwise be described as entangled and capable of coherent connection in the sense that quantum theory describes as "strange" or "spooky" "action at a distance." In the ordinary terms I am using, the soul does not move so much as simply become itself in relationship to the body. These distinctions find more importance in relationship to the traditional notions of, for example, "being out of body," "shamanic journeying," "astral projection," and "protection." When the soul is in coherent relationship with the body, it can experience and perform all of these functions but do so while remaining in fully supportive relationship with the body. The soul, in my construct, need not "leave," since its nature is not to move, but to tune itself and then tune to those other fields with which it experiences coherent relation. To shift identity to the soul, we also have to shift from the older metaphors that informed our understandings to new metaphors that allow for larger understandings and the skills associated with that larger view.

*Continuing now to the next step, expand your radiant light so that the light surrounds the body already filled with your light, forming up a womb-like container made of light that extends from the body a distance of perhaps one meter. Now, the body is interpenetrated and surrounded by your light, while you continue to hold yourself in a completely focused, present manner with nothing else in your field of awareness other than this relationship with the body.*

*Remembering that you are a drop of the singular consciousness of which the cosmos consists, feather out a filament of your own light from the edge of the womb with which you have surrounded the body. Extend your filament to your home in heaven, from which you came to reside in the body. The body is the soul's home away from home for the lifetime of the body. The soul always remains connected to its home of origin. The body/mind will not know the way, but you remember the way. With an intention to return to that home, imagine your way home and, finding yourself there in the instant facilitated by intention and imagination, take a moment to remember your source and re-experience the feeling of home.*

You will notice that the metaphor of this description resorts to the notion that the soul is itself disconnected and must reach out to re-connect. This is the source of the metaphor that the soul "forgets" who it is as it initially enters the body. These are time-space metaphors, so I have continued in that vein, even though a more sophisticated view is that the soul is always connected but temporarily out of tune. With that more sophisticated view, if one can call it that, the soul merely concentrates itself and knows its inherent nature, which is being a part of all that exists, which provides that sense of home to a mental perspective that assumes disconnection in a time-space sense. Whether to engage this more quantum perspective depends entirely on whether it will help the client find an understanding, or metaphor, that works.

> *Then, returning your focus to the womb with which you have surrounded the body, focus upon the breath. With that breath, draw the love of heaven into yourself, intensifying the field you have created around the body, and, with the next exhalation, breathe this divine love into the body. Fill the soul with that love, then breathe it out into the body.*
>
> *Repeat this breath several times until you begin to have the sense that the body is being flooded with heaven's light, which is no more or less than the light of which the soul is made.*

Using the information I am getting directly from the body, I determine whether the client is connecting or struggling. I check in with the client as necessary if it feels like there is some resistance. The check in may be "How are you doing?" or "What are you experiencing?" If things are moving forward, we continue. If not, we stop and address whatever needs to be addressed.

> *Now, feather out a second filament of your own light from the field you have formed as the body's container. With intention and imagination, extend this*

*filament to the heart of the earth. The body/mind will*
*not know the way, but the soul knows the way.*

Preceding the session, I have explained that my experience
has given rise to an understanding that earth itself has a body,
a soul, and a heart—that it is a living being like ourselves—a
body ensouled through a heart that emanates the love of heaven
into the earth body. Like the heaven dimensions, the earth
radiates a love by which it conveys its nature as Mother of all
earth-based life. My own experience of the earth's love is that it
has a different texture, perhaps one of a slower vibration that is
more available to the body's vibratory range without the necessity of the greater stepping down of frequencies that is involved
in the process of the body finding a harmony with the higher
frequencies emanating from what I have called the "heaven"
dimensions.

> *Contemplate that the earth being has anticipated*
> *your reaching out to re-connect mother's love to its*
> *child—your body—from which it was disconnected as*
> *the body formed in the arms of a heaven-sent soul and*
> *the womb of a human mother.*
>
> *Allow yourself to feel deeply into the nature of this*
> *earth-mother love, so distinct but no less powerful or*
> *deep than the love that is heaven-sent by and through*
> *the soul that you are.*
>
> *Then connect your filament to the heart of the*
> *earth with the blessing of the Mother and return your*
> *focus to the soul-field by which you contain the body.*
> *With your next breath, breathe in the love of the earth*
> *through your filament, fill your soul-self, and breathe*
> *the unconditional love of earth out into the body,*
> *flooding the body with Mother's love.*
>
> *Repeat this breath several times until you begin to*
> *have the body sense that it is being flooded with the*
> *light of both heaven and earth.*

*Continuing, breathe in the love of heaven and the love of earth simultaneously, continuing to flood the body with love. Notice how the body responds as you continue to breathe deeply, slowly, gently, and silently.*

\*\*\*

This is the foundational practice. There are certainly many ways to visualize the pathways of the breath that facilitate the otherwise complex matter of understanding how we might take in the love of heaven and earth simultaneously, but you will find your own way of doing it. There is a particular way that I have been shown to do in the initiations and ceremonies that have led me to this practice. I share that way with clients, but I do not presume that there are not many ways to experience this connection between soul, body, and the other dimensions that foster our work on the planet.

This foundational practice should be done daily in the time that you have set aside for meditation. Although what I have described can take ten or fifteen minutes as you focus on each element in turn, I have found that, with practice, I can bring the entire practice together in a few seconds, after which I continue the practice from the point at which the above narration ended for about thirty minutes. With practice, this routine moves into the background and becomes automatic. Moving the practice into the background allows room for the three intelligences of knowing, thinking, and visioning to operate within the open space that is created as the body begins to feel the sense of safety that a heightened state of love creates in the body. As the body's sense of safety increases, it allows the soul to move in more and more, so that the soul has access to the body's assistance for doing the soul's work.

There is a quote I have heard attributed to the Dalai Lama, but have been unable to find, that describes this process in a practical way. Asked what he does when he meditates, the Dalai Lama was said to have replied he plans his day. This is what I do. With this soul process operating with the body in the background of the collaborative intelligences at work, purpose reveals itself in discrete next steps. *Ah, this is what I need to do next,* I realize. Sometimes words come for a poem. Sometimes concepts come for my writing. Sometimes, I think of who it is I need to call and connect with. Sometimes I feel the direct presence of a guide. Sometimes I feel something that does not operate in language, something like a pressure or presence, calling my attention to attend for a while longer. Sometimes there is a vision, or a hint of a vision. All the while, in the background of these emergences, my soul holds the body in the gentle breath of love.

In the next chapter, I will describe how I take the client to a next step on the massage table, one that I call the "body retrieval."

# 14

# FROM SOUL RETRIEVAL TO BODY RETRIEVAL

## *Why We Heal*

MANY OF US THINK OF HEALING as something we do to stop pain, remediate a physical limitation, or cure a disease so that we can get back to what we were doing before we couldn't do it anymore. But a soul perspective suggests a greater outcome for healing—that healing is the means to getting traction on the job we came to do here on the planet. Otherwise, drugs and surgery might do the job of healing just as well. Indeed, our conventional medical system seems content with stopping pain without great concern for its ultimate origin. And, in a very direct way, the origin of much of our pain is our failure to understand who we are and why we came to the planet. From a soul perspective, pain and suffering were designed into the human system to awaken the soul by making us focus our attention on what needs to be healed. Focusing attention is also how we come into direct contact with our soul nature.

Ordinary physical injury is a familiar challenge. When our pain is great enough, we either pay attention to its source, or risk an eventual disability or death. However, the ultimate source of suffering is disconnection from who we are, our inattention to the work we came to do, and our failure to attend to the means of doing it.

So, from a soul perspective, healing serves several objectives, in sequence. First, pain differentiates the soul from the body by the mechanism of dissociation. It gets the soul out where we can experience the soul as separate from the body.

Second, pain takes us to the location of the trauma in the body and the events in the body's timeline that caused the trauma. Quite apart from taking us to the address of physical maladies, this focus on location and event provides the opportunity to learn how our early trauma has created a pattern of beliefs that formed our strategic defenses against the world—beliefs that need to be dropped in favor of more functional understandings.

Third, shifting a preoccupation of our attention from the body to the world allows the soul to use the senses of the body to connect its gift to the world with purpose.

Lastly, as the body feels safe enough to turn its attention with openness to the world, it also is better able to access the life force that fuels its physicality in service of the soul's purpose.

## What Healing Is

Once we are clear on why we heal—from a soul perspective—it is easier to see what healing requires.

The first step is to form a preliminary hypothesis—a provisional understanding—that our objective is not merely to stop pain and suffering, but to use the pain and suffering as the very pathway toward our eventual healing.

Second, a soul perspective suggests that soul can take the lead in our healing. With this perspective, we can see that the initial objective of healing is to differentiate the soul from the body and strengthen it so that it can lead in the subsequent stages of healing the body.

Third, as the soul is able to take the lead in our healing, we are able to shift focus to the body itself and follow the pain to its source, rather than numb the pain or dissociate from it.

Fourth, as we come to the source of our pain, we find that early events formed beliefs that formed strategies that formed behaviors that crashed into the world. Then we have a place to work where meaningful change can occur.

Lastly, our healing represents a confluence of events: a recognition that our early trauma was—at its root—an experience of disconnection; an event of reconnection of sufficient magnitude to communicate to the body its capability of feeling safe in the world; the clearing of old beliefs and the substitution of new understandings that represent a soul perspective on the relationship of soul and body to the world; the development of skill sufficient to cultivate and maintain an experience of connection for the body that creates an ongoing sense of relative safety in the world; and the development of skill sufficient to use the now available sensuality of the body to connect the soul's gift to coherent opportunities churned up daily by an ever changing world.

Albert Einstein's familiar maxim that you can't solve a problem with the same kind of thinking you used to create it is applicable here. It is not enough just to shift thinking or take on a new belief. I've said that a soul perspective must ultimately arise not from belief or thinking, but from experience. That is what Einstein's maxim means in this context. You have to shift from thinking to experience.

But, at the very beginning, we have to use thinking to get the idea that the first step is to loosen our old thinking—our old beliefs—enough to get to a new experience. So we start with the idea that there *is* a clear objective for humans, that we have a purpose, and that you are part of that purpose. That soul perspective suggests that our purpose as humans is to play a key role in an ongoing and open-ended planetary creation and that you are hard-wired to pursue that purpose. It's what calls to you. I've invited you to try this perspective on in your consciousness and see if you resonate with it. If so, it's a frame you can start with, a way of orienting as you move away from any sense of confusion, pain, or frustration that caused you to pick up yet one more book.

## Healing the Soul First

When we first attend our pain, we discover the difficulty we have staying present to it. As much as we experience pain, we also experience a separation. And, in that separation, we find the lever for our work—the soul itself. We find soul in the experience of seeing ourselves as observer, as the one who distances from pain, as the one who thinks about the pain.

In our meditation traditions, we find the tools to strengthen the soul from the juncture of that insight gained in the awareness of separation, even if those traditions do not see soul as real. *I am not this pain, or these thoughts, or this body,* we recite to ourselves. We use pain, thoughts, and body to learn how to focus attention as a thing in itself. And my soul perspective says simply, give that focused attention a name. Let's call that the *soul.* It is a place to stand. It is not a belief, but an experience. But remember, when we have separated that attention from the pain, the soul is largely out of the body.

These same meditation traditions suggest an omega point, often called oneness or the non-dual state. Before the omega point is an experience for you, it is a thought, a possibility, and possibly a belief. Go there, if you like, experience that dissolution. There is value there. However, from a soul perspective, it is not an end, but only an intermediate point. You can let yourself return with all the strength of attention that took you there and bring that attention back to the intermediate point between the body and that omega point. Feel into yourself. Ask, not whether you are the omega point, but whether you sense a purpose in the direction of the body and the planet. Feel the momentum of this focal point of attention I am calling soul when you have the strength to be neither body nor omega point.

If you are not a strong meditator, then let us begin this work in another way. That is what I use my coaching and the massage table for. This is assisted meditation. It is a place to start. As we observe that the pain has pushed the attention/soul from the body, we have a place to start. Either way, our first objective is to strengthen the soul and allow it to be a thing in itself.

So long as we limit our efforts at healing to the thinking that disabled us—so long as we work inside the system that is the very source of our pain—we will remain caught in the confusion that is itself our most painful distraction. We can't pull ourselves up, another saying assumes, by our own bootstraps. But differentiating the soul from the body allows us to identify ourselves as soul and pull the body up from there. In finding our soul nature, we find that we are, indeed, separate from the body that experiences pain. Pain is the fulcrum, and soul the lever by which we lift the body in the direction of health.

The soul is far easier to "heal" than the body. The soul is pure consciousness. It can be diffuse or focused. To render the soul whole and capable, we need merely focus it. Focusing the soul means that we gather it back—retrieve it—from where it has gone outside the body and also hidden in the body. Pain is a wonderful motivation to do that. Pain "catches" our attention and brings it to a single point of focus. Once we learn how to focus attention without the aid of an external motivator such as pain, it is a simple step to learn that it can be placed wherever the soul chooses. When the soul becomes focused, it is capable of situating itself in the heart portal, from which the soul accesses the fulcrum of pain upon which the soul's lever can begin to pry the body out of its deep hole.

It is this understanding that has moved my own practice away from the notion of soul retrievals as it is often taught in the modern shamanism movement. That view assumes the soul to be fragile. Trauma, it is thought, fragments the soul. There is the additional view that the fragile soul flees the body's pain. I would suggest another view: the deeper cause of dissociation is that a traumatized body pushes the soul out of the body to minimize the pain. The soul is neutral to the contents of its awareness. The body is not. When soul is present, the body will experience the pain of its trauma.

Additionally, the current view of shamanic teaching seems to be that the mere presence of the soul in the body is sufficient to heal the human system, hence the emphasis on retrieving it. What this view neglects is the recognition that getting soul into the body is not the complete solution, but only the first step in a much more complicated piece of work in healing the body itself. We have to recognize that the body is not ready to receive the soul if it was what pushed the soul out in the first place, and that fragments of the soul are scattered throughout the body as well as outside it, lodged in the unconsciously held historic traumas.

What I concluded about traditional soul retrievals is that it is not difficult for a healer to bring that focus of attention back into the heart of a client in so tangible a way that it can be felt in the moment. And it can have effects for the moments that attention remains. During that time, insights can arise that power decisions of import. I have had that experience with a soul retrieval performed for me by another healer. It allowed me to move past a particular barrier in that moment of my life. But, as also I experienced with my own clients, such a retrieval does not last long, and the issues that preceded the retrieval often reconstellate—perhaps in a different form or diminished force, but they can return nevertheless.

The ultimate soul retrieval is one that you have to do for yourself. And that consists of your developing the *skill* that is represented by learning how to focus attention and where to place it to accomplish the variety of tasks a focused soul can accomplish. Then you can get to work on the body in a far more effective way, becoming the partner of those healers who can ally with your soul in service of bringing the body to the level of function necessary to partner with your soul. Among those healers that the soul can access are the entheogenic plant medicines, and I will speak of those alliances in the next chapter.

So, I say, soul first. That is the easy part. Fix the soul by learning to pay attention. Then learn where to place that attention. Then fix the body with the soul. In other words, retrieve the soul from its external haunts. Retrieving the body—and the soul parts that remain hidden in the body—with the focused soul comes next.

## Shifting Focus to the Body

In Chapter Two, I spoke about how the body carries all its experience as an accumulating memory, the totality of which constitutes the body's now. All of us experience trauma to one degree or another, and we interpret the world through the lens of our trauma. The trauma may result in observable physical injuries, or it may not. Either way, such injuries define how we interpret our relationship with the world. Our interpretations of our woundings are the source of understandings and beliefs we develop and control how we navigate the world.

Our interpretations can go in two fundamentally different ways. We can understand our trauma as evidence that we are victims of an uncaring world in which our survival demands our constant vigilance. Or we can understand our continuing trauma as evidence that we don't understand our relationship with the world and that we need to get a better understanding. If we are not going to continue as victims, we need to consider that our understandings and beliefs are based in a misinterpretation of the nature of the world and our place in it. If we continue to embrace beliefs that are the substance of a victim perspective, we cannot embrace the world, and the world cannot embrace us.

So long as we carry beliefs that separate us from the world, we cannot transform and integrate our early victim experiences. So long as those experiences remain unintegrated, they remain raw and continue to traumatize the body. There are two consequences of remaining closed to new experience. First, the body remains unavailable to the soul. Second, the body is also closed to the life force that emanates from the earth. Without access to that life force, the body's battery depletes. Exhaustion, depression, and illness follow naturally. In order to have full access to life force, the body must open to the experience of connection. To do that, we have to release old beliefs that block positive experience, and adopt understandings that allow positive experience to occur. A soul perspective is such an understanding, yet we can come to it only through experience. Switching beliefs does not help.

Healing is not an erasure of traumatic memories. It is rather a welcoming home of those experiences, a holding of those memories in the space of love. It is a way of discovering why our personalities have become what they are. It is a way of understanding why we do what we do, what drives us, and what causes us to react.

Nor is healing an elimination of all reaction. Healing allows for a diminishment of reaction—in the space of safety provided by the soul's focused presence—to a level that allows us to recognize the role of earlier trauma in our behaviors of the moment. Ram Dass speaks of inviting our old emotional reactions in for tea, rendering them into little schmoozes. I would add that we invite them in for a purpose: they are very smart schmoozes. We need to listen to what they have to say and elicit the lessons from our old experience, including how we have misinterpreted it and how we are tempted to continue our misinterpretations. Healing drops the defenses and denial we have around trauma, not the traumatic experiences themselves. Healing then holds those traumatic experiences within the space of safety and love, diminishing their destructive power, but not their instructive presence. Healing is the substitution of the wisdom that is distilled by the soul from the prior experience that was misinterpreted by an immature consciousness.

Although we need not erase the memories of early trauma, we do need to release the beliefs that formed as a consequence of those traumatic events. In *The Soul's Critical Path,* I described how, as a three-year-old, I was the audience for my mother's outbursts of fear and anger. Something in me realized that, were I to trigger such behavior in my mother, I would not be safe in the world. My immature mind strategized, quite unconsciously, that my survival would depend on the approval of other people. I formed a belief that it was not safe to express my own feelings or behave in ways that were not acceptable to others. That unconscious belief lodged itself so firmly that it controlled my behaviors well into my fifth decade. I continued long into adulthood to seek the approval of others and to modify my behaviors to get that approval at the same time I hid behaviors I felt to be unacceptable—in effect splitting myself. I continued those behaviors despite a continuing failure to get the love that my body sought as the substance of connection for which it yearned. The eventual process of my healing allowed the memory of my mother's outbursts to rise to the surface along with the feeling of fear that my body still carried in response to that early experience. By finding a sense of relative physical safety through the experiences of connection I have described in my books, the body was able to release this early, unconscious belief even though I continue to carry the memory of the events themselves. That healing not only resolved the split within myself, but my relationship with my mother.

As I compare my memory of this early sense of disconnection to the abuse so many children have suffered at the hands of others, I have often thought my early experience to be relatively insignificant. Yet, I was able at one point to witness a depth of my own hidden response to trauma that my conscious memory had been unable to access. There was a day in my early forties that I participated in a role-playing session with a group I had been working with for a few months. My assignment was to speak my truth to my spouse, who was not in the workshop. Her role would be played by a female volunteer. As I faced the woman and opened my mouth to speak, the woman instantly morphed into my mother. Before I could utter even a few words, my vision tunneled, and my entire body was seized by tetany—an involuntary seizing of the muscles—causing me to become completely numb and fall tree-like to the floor. The seizure lasted for half an hour, during which any touch by those attempting to help me was accompanied by excruciating pain. Something had happened in my childhood, if only by accretion, to bring me to an early belief about the nature of the world as hostile. At the time of that event, I was otherwise fully functional in my life, conducting a successful law practice and raising a family, quite unaware of the depth of this dark undercurrent that kept me in a state of continuing disconnection. In retrospect, I can see that I was living in a continual state of dissociation and depression of which I only gradually became aware as my healing process progressed.

That single, early belief that my safety was dependent upon others, combined with an experience of disconnection, spawned many other beliefs. For example, it was easy to believe that I was not worthy of love, that I had to earn love, that love came only from other people, and so on. As we begin to work through our beliefs, we will find that they originate with just a few core beliefs. When we are able to identify these core beliefs by discovering their particular location in the body, we can more quickly unravel the beliefs by which we explained our original experiences to ourselves. The belief that we are simply bodies, for example, easily leads to the additional beliefs that we are ultimately vulnerable, disconnected, and alone. When we experience ourselves as souls and recognize how the soul can care for the body, then our beliefs relating to loneliness and vulnerability can more easily be released. This is the essence of healing the body.

Healing the body calls upon a shift in consciousness that recognizes—from integrating deep experiences of connection—that we are not only connected, but connected to a world of mystery that feeds, loves, and supports us without the necessity of our understanding *what* it is so much as the necessity of understanding *that* it is. We need only understand how to acknowledge it, connect to it, and work with it.

In short, healing is about locating the core beliefs, disrupting their hold on the body long enough with an experience of deep connection, integrating the experience of connection into a new understanding of our relationship with the world, developing the skill to maintain the experience of connection, then partnering body with soul. In this process, the toxic effects of the original and ongoing trauma can dissipate and be reduced to an instructional memory—an event from which we have learned our lesson.

## How We Invite and Integrate the Healing

There is a point at which the relationship between the body and the soul begins to shift. Over time, a daily practice by the soul of flooding the body with love causes the body to respond and turn its attention to the soul. This stage of relationship between soul and body is similar to the stage of relationship that occurs when two people begin to feel an attraction to one another. They discover that there is a connection between them. There is a shift in focus. They begin to pay attention to each other with increasing interest, even though they are not yet capable of a fully skilled, intimate relationship.

As this new stage of relationship begins to get momentum, the soul takes the lead. When the body expresses the pain of disconnection, it is the soul that is called to respond. With this call from the body, the soul has the opportunity to recognize that it needs to awaken, strengthen itself, and find traction on the planet by connecting its gift to opportunity and opportunity to purpose. So the soul tends to itself first, which is the process for which we begin to use meditation, medicine plants, vision quests, "enlightenment" processes, and any technique that helps the soul to differentiate itself from the body. As the airplane steward explains, you need to put your own oxygen mask on first, then put one on the child. The body is initially as a wild child to the maturing soul. It is the soul that leads by learning how to focus attention. This is why, even when we begin to learn how to meditate, we experience the relief that comes from the soul dissociating from the body even though our trauma remains fully present and captures our attention once more as our meditation session ends. Meditation, in its initial stages, only serves to strengthen the soul and teach us the skill of focusing attention. We have to practice meditation to acquire the skill to take the next step. It is this juncture to which the next step of the process applies, the step that this chapter describes.

In the prior chapter, I described a visualization that brings the soul to a strong self-focus and the shift of identity that allows the soul to see itself as distinct from the body. In that visualization, I also described how this newly focused soul begins to flood the body with love. The practice of this visualization over time creates the opportunity for the soul to actually *experience* itself as a distinct entity. This is not about belief. The experience gives rise to the new thought—a cognition—that is tantamount to a shift in identity from that sense that you are some combination of body and personality with a soul drifting around somewhere. Now, you experience yourself as a soul more and more and know yourself to be an active agent independent from but deeply connected to your body. As identity shifts in this way, so does the personality, which is a mirror of the thoughts that arise from your experience, just as it was a mirror of the thoughts that formerly arose from your prior beliefs. But now, you have abandoned the process of belief and adopted the process of personal experience as you become a self-identified, strong, and focused soul.

Even as the soul makes significant changes for itself, the body will not have caught up to these changes. The body remains in an unconsciously traumatized state, with its brain/mind not completely aware of how the trauma resides secretly in the body, speaking only through the ground state of anxiety and stress that characterize the lives of so many of us. It is such a body to which the soul begins to address its newly enlarged capacity for flooding the body with love. It is that flood of love to which the anxious, stressed body begins to respond as it turns its attention to the soul as the source of this loving attention.

That next step is for the newly focused soul to help the body address its trauma. In Chapter Two, I talked about the body's "now," which is a historic timeline that includes the memory of all that has happened to the body during its lifetime. This now may include traumatic events that have occurred in prior lifetimes that find their way, in some way, to the body of this lifetime. Even as the soul continues for the body's lifetime the baseline activity of flooding the body with love, the soul now takes this next step of healing the body from within its timeline by the soul becoming its own shaman.

In shamanic traditions, healers use intention and imagination to take out-of-body journeys for a variety of specific purposes. These journeys gather information, communicate with the higher self of the shaman's client and with helper spirit guides, retrieve the errant soul of the client so that it can return to the body, evoke the help of spirit guides, and so on. In the process I am describing here, the soul itself is taking the place of the third-person healer or shaman. It is the soul that becomes the active agent for healing the body. With the process I have already described, *the soul has retrieved itself.* The soul has already placed itself in the center of the chest of its own body and done what a shaman cannot do for a client: the soul has become the active agent of flooding love into its body on a daily basis, so that the body is never without the love of heaven and earth. Without that arrangement, the weakly ensouled body must make a periodic appointment with a healer to get an energy injection and perhaps bring the unfocused and drifting soul back to the body. Now, with a self-identified soul taking up intentional residence in the heart portal, the third-party healer becomes unnecessary except in times of crisis, when even a focused, self-identified soul becomes overwhelmed in such a way that focus is lost. It happens, but it happens less and less as the soul becomes stronger and more intentional in its relationship with the body. This is the way that we become our own teachers and healers, cutting the cord from the pattern of moving through life dependent upon one or several teachers. This is literally how we are evolving away from the master/guru/priest paradigm of spiritual growth. We are coming to a place of collaborating with other healers for our own healing, becoming interdependent rather than codependent.

Here's how this second step by which the self-identified soul—as shaman to its own body—can begin. The journey is taken in the timeline of the body.

This stage of work follows the guided visualization described in the last chapter. It is seldom part of the first session with a new client. When the client is ready, I add this piece. It continues on the massage table, as I support the creation of a deeper state of relaxation by coaching the client in the breathing technique and by holding the client's head with the cranial/sacral technique. I speak softly to the client:

> *Continue to breathe deeply, slowly, gently, and silently. Give a little attention to the process of breathing, but give your greater attention to what we are about to do.*
>
> *Using intention and imagination, shift your attention to the moment of the body's conception.*

Prior to the table session, I have explained to the client about the body's timeline. In the original event of soul coming together with the event of conception, the soul became merged into the body, losing any semblance of self-awareness. But now, the soul has regained its self-awareness and becomes present to witness both conception and the soul's former state in the process of initial merger, using the body's sensual memory of that event. Because the soul is not a creature of time, it can dip into any juncture of time. The body could be said to *be* time.

> *Let yourself simply be present to this event. As you move through the heart portal, the body's sensuality becomes available to you. With the body's senses, you can be aware of the feeling of this historic event of soul arrival and fetal conception. Take your time and observe.*

As I guide a client through this process, I ask that the client narrate his or her experiences to me. This serves more than one purpose. First, it keeps the client awake, since the state of relaxation within which this process occurs disposes people to fall asleep. If this were simply a healing session, I would encourage sleep. But this process is focused not on healing as a primary outcome, but upon *learning* how the soul facilitates healing in the body day by day as the process is applied by the client over time

Second, the client's narration bookmarks for the client significant events that occur during the session; this happens simply by the necessity of putting events into words. When the client has been silent for as long as a couple of minutes, I may say, "What are you experiencing now?" I may ask the question many times during a session. I watch the time. I listen to the client's responses. I feel what is happening in the client's body. I watch for wavering attention and tiredness. With all of this information, I assess whether the client, as soul, has engaged the body's timeline at a sufficient level to have encountered a raw, experiential engagement with the body's hidden information. From experience, I know that a single piece of information during a session is a nugget in the pan. No need to push the river or dredge the whole thing. Further sessions, with the coach or on your own, will reveal more. So I use the question to bring that nugget to the surface. Nevertheless, I caution the client not to move from this process of engaging raw experience into a process of thinking—of trying to understand what is happening. It is a subtle but important distinction. We keep the words to a minimum.

Third, the client's narration allows me to hear about the significant events so that I can help the client remember what happened in the rarefied consciousness that the session represents. If the client tries to remember everything that has happened while on the massage table, the raw experience becomes less available.

Fourth, as the client is working, I am also getting relevant information in another way. The client's narration allows me some confirmation of what I am feeling. Sometimes, I will get a vision, the simple sensation of a shift in energy, or a palpable shift in the cerebral spinal fluid pulse. These events tell me something is happening in the body's consciousness. In such an event, I can choose to ask the client what is happening in order to bring the client's attention to that moment, when the client may have missed it, or simply because we can give some emphasis to the event. The client is working in a dreamlike state, which is in its own way disorienting to the linear mind, so a collaboration between coach and client is important in bringing information back at the end of the session.

Because I am working with the client as a soul sitting within the heart portal of my own body, with the intention to follow the client's soul in this journey into the timeline of the client's body, I can often feel what is happening. It is not unusual for a client's soul to assume the significant focus that is the desired eventual outcome of this process, if only for the time that the client is on the massage table. When that happens, it is easy for me to feel the power of that soul actually enter the client's body and fill the entire room. When that happens, I know that we are making progress, and I share that information with the client at the end of the session.

*Continuing, focus your attention upon observing the event of soul and fetal body merging at the moment of conception. Take your time. Simply be present.*

This is the most challenging aspect of the process: maintaining soul focus in an unfamiliar arena, not knowing what to expect while working not to expect anything at all. For myself, as a coach, it is also critical that I not have expectations. I know that there are times and layers. The soul's presence at a moment in the timeline of the body may not evoke any experience at all on a particular day because the layer at which the body's memory is held may not be accessible on a particular day. The reason for the unavailability may be that the trauma is more deeply held; it needs more than the relative sense of safety that the body feels during a particular session can make available. So, on a particular day, the attention moves on.

Over time, the process consists of the soul beginning at the beginning of the body's timeline and drifting slowing forward, seeing what comes up. It is not unlike a woodworker who begins to sand a piece of word. After the first sanding, the woodworker feels the wood with his or her hand to see what the first sanding has accomplished. Then more sanding follows, followed by more feeling. Eventually, the wood has become smooth to the touch. In the same way, the soul continues to move over historical timeframes in the body's history, feeling for metaphorical roughness—the sensation that signals the buried trauma-treasure that it seeks to reveal. The soul's presence is the sandpaper, becoming more and more soft as it works toward an ultimate smoothness of sensation.

I know, and emphasize to the client, that none of this work on the massage table is of much ultimate value unless the client integrates the work by the discipline of a daily practice that repeats the process until it becomes automatic. When the client begins to experience a shift in the ground state of the body such that the prevailing state of anxiety and stress has diminished noticeably, then the next stage of work can begin in earnest.

How can we characterize this shift? I like to say that there is a point at which the wild body turns its head toward the soul, recognizing the soul as its soulmate. The way that a body experiences this recognition is very different than the way in which the soul knows and acknowledges this relationship. When the wild body knows its mate, it falls in love with its soul, with all of the passion that attends the falling in love that most of us have been fortunate enough to experience. The soul side of that event is perhaps more dry, but the body side of that event is a huge energetic event. Still, the soul can share in the grand joy of that feeling because it reads the sensuality of the body in all of its experience.

The soul accesses this sensuality of the body by *merging* into it. Merger is the mechanism by which the soul works in collaboration with the heart portal. The heart, as described in earlier chapters, works by resonance, merging through coherence with other fields, subtle and material. This is precisely how the soul is able to move in the body's timeline. By flooding the body with the love of heaven and earth, the soul brings coherence to the body's incoherent ground state. As the body comes to a state of coherence, it is able to make its senses fully available to the soul. Without body coherence, the soul is able only to experience the incoherence of the body. Without further sanding, so to say, the soul can only know that the body is not ready for prime time, and the soul will have to do further work before it can use the body more completely and efficiently to engage the soul's purpose in the world.

But when the body itself becomes coherent—when the body's traumas have been largely integrated and the body has found the ground state of an abiding sense of safety in relationship to the focused soul and therefore to the world itself—then the body is ready for the next step, which is making its senses and feet available to the soul in seeking its purpose in the world.

## Journeying Outside the Body

Before I leave the matter of journeying as a technique for healing, I want to say a few words about journeying outside the body.

Years before I learned the technique of journeying in the body's timeline, I facilitated journeys "outside" of the body for my clients, both on the massage table and otherwise. Using the techniques taught by modern shamanic teachers, I would use an imaginary jumping off point or an actual destination. Such a destination, for example, was the Temple of the Moon above Cusco in southern Peru. In both cases, the objective of the journey was to obtain information and healing by connecting with other-dimensional spirit helpers.

My clients ordinarily received both a sense of connection and insight from such journeys. For many of these clients, these journeys represented their first experience with other-dimensional encounters. Even though there was benefit accruing from that process, my own guidance from such spirit helpers suggested that we were not getting to the deeper healing for these clients. We were working not without regard for the traumas of the body, but away from the body nevertheless.

I continue to see value in these out-of-body journeys, for exactly what they have accomplished in terms of the experience of connection and insight. However, I have largely discontinued that practice in favor of the practice of journeying in the timeline of the body, since it accomplishes the experience of connection, insight, *and* direct encounters with the traumas of the body exactly where those traumas reside. I feel that the resultant healings are more effective.

Part of what caused me to make this shift in technique was a shift in understanding about how the soul journeys. The soul is not a point in time, or a discrete physical thing. It is a field. In that sense, it has the capacity to be omnipresent. As I described in the previous chapter, the soul can center itself in the heart portal and do all of its work by *expansion.* I recognize that the notion of centering a field in the heart and expanding is itself a metaphorical way of speaking of a field that does neither. However, by using the metaphor and imagining our simultaneously holding the soul in the heart portal and expanding the soul, we can better catch the experience of journeying beyond the body without leaving it. That allows us to pay attention to the body while we also reach beyond it to receive the experience of connection with and insight from other-dimensional beings who support our spiritual work.

What I have found is that journeys focused upon the timeline of the body encounter these out-of-body beings anyway. In other words, the timeline journeys accomplish the work of the more traditional out-of-body journeys while working more deeply within the body itself. I also have some concern that, among the other-dimensional fields available to our journeys, some are less valuable for our healing than others. When we work from the body, I sense that there is a greater capacity for a coherent heart to constellate the most coherent other-dimensional fields—an opportunity that we may lose if we are journeying outside the body rather than from within it.

The same distinction of journeying in or out of the body applies when plant medicines are involved, and I will digress to talk about how those medicines affect this healing process in the next chapter before coming finally to the process of finding soul purpose in the final chapter.

# 15

# A ROLE FOR PLANT MEDICINES AND OTHER HEALERS

AFTER I FIRST ENCOUNTERED AYAHUASCA in Peru and got a taste of its power, I asked the shaman a question that was more important than I could understand then. It remains even now an important question. I had been working consciously on a spiritual path for at least fifteen years before that encounter. "Is the medicine necessary?" I asked. "Can we do what the medicine does without the medicine?"

Without hesitation, he said, "Of course you can." It was a generous answer, but not a sufficient one. He was making the medicine his life's work for a reason. And he didn't suggest the alternative pathway. In retrospect, I doubt that he understood an alternative pathway, nor did he appear, as I worked with him over time, to have resolved some basic personality issues that limited his ability to facilitate his clients' processes. When I asked the question, I did not have any understanding of the destination that I presumed to exist—an omega point that represents what the plant medicine can "do"—nor did I have any idea of a process such as the one I have subsequently developed and expressed in this book. And I certainly didn't have anything like a full view of the medicine's capacity to do the healing that facilitates great change and opens doorways.

Fifteen years later, I have worked with ayahuasca and other plant medicines enough to have at least a partial answer to my own question. My answer would be this: I don't know if you can do without the medicines what you can do with them. Some of you may be able to. I think I have come to a place in my life journey that was not otherwise likely for me without the intervention of the medicines.

During the same period of time, I have had occasion to work with a number of healers as well. Certainly, some healers are more effective than others. Observing more powerful healers, I can see a parallel between the work of the plant medicines and the work that such healers do. To fully explore that relationship would be an undertaking far beyond the scope of this book. However, I want to comment briefly upon the relationship between the work of the plant medicines, healers, and the process I've described in this book.

My experience with the plant medicines suggests that the encounter with plants *in ceremony*—there is no other rational approach to using these medicines—involves several things going on at one time. First, the medicines push into the body in a way that is difficult though not impossible to resist, which is precisely why we use them. The defensive patterns with which a body adapts to historical trauma often resist any attempt at intervention, whether it is talk therapy, healing energies, or the plant medicine. Because the medicine is so pushy, the plant medicines tend to be more powerful than any but the most powerful of human healers.

Second, the medicine typically facilitates a sense of safety in the body that inclines the body to receive the medicine's intervention. This may not occur with a first encounter with a medicine as forceful as ayahuasca since it can easily trigger the body's defenses at the same time it tends to overrun them. I imagine that any healer must also address the need for a sense of safety in order to dispose the body to receive the healing.

Third, with the opening of the body made possible by the intervention of the medicine, the body becomes available to the further intervention by healing spirits or fields of intelligence that would, without the medicine, not have direct access to the body to do their healing work. In the same way, powerful healers act as a channel for such other-dimensional spirits or fields that do the actual healing, but they also have to get beyond the body's defenses.

I sense that this basic process occurs with all of the plant medicines and other forms of healing. Whether the ultimate healing work is done through the facilitation of the plant medicine or a healer, both open the door by facilitating safety and linking the body to other-dimensional healers.

What is often missing in these healing encounters, however, is a way for the client to *integrate* the healing. Shifting a pathological condition does not, in and of itself, prevent the condition from arising again. Cancer, for example, may be a symptom of any number of causal factors that may remain present even when the tumor is removed. Defensive patterns that arise from trauma can persist even if the pain caused by the trauma is temporarily relieved. Healing alone does not provide the skill-based process that allows the client to take that next step. That next step involves a process and understanding such as I have described at length in this book. Situating a self-identified soul in the heart portal and pumping love into the body before a healing is accessed predisposes the body to open to the effects of healing and also creates a process that will prevent a condition from reconstellating.

I suspect that the process I have described in this book is sufficient in itself, without intervention by a plant or other healer, to eventually bring about the body's healing. However, I feel it works more powerfully and quickly when combined with the deep healing that plant medicines and powerful healers can initiate. Moreover, the process I have described makes the healings more effective when you can combine the process and healings simultaneously. In other words, learning the process prepares one for the healing, helps the healing to go deeper by the ability to receive it more skillfully in the first place, and helps complete the healing by integrating the lesson of the trauma after the healing occurs. In my other books, I have said that the common encounter with the plant medicine in Peru often fails to produce long-term consequences because of the absence of a process of preparation, support, and integration. What I have described in this book is that process.

There is another reason that a process that parallels the work of healers and healing plants is important. The medicines and other healers open doorways to experiences and relationships with other-dimensional beings that have an existence independent of the medicine itself. Those relationships, like relationships with other humans, are unpredictable learning journeys unto themselves. Every ceremony I have is a new encounter. I learn something new almost every time. New relationships arise from time to time. Another shaman confirmed the same to me just a few years ago. After decades of work with his particular medicine, he said that he learned something in every ceremony. The guide relationship evolves. As I've learned to integrate my healings with process, I've found that I can sometimes connect with the other-dimensional healers and guides directly, without the intervention of the medicine. So the medicine and other powerful healers kick-start an open-ended process leading toward an ever-receding horizon toward which we are propelled not only by our desire for healing, but by the grandness of human curiosity and our inbuilt desire to create. With this skill-based process, we are propelled into a larger relationship with the cosmos and its possibilities, aided by the skill to find our purpose within the space of those possibilities.

To ask whether the medicine is necessary to the work, we need to be clear about what the work is. The answer to that is, of necessity, also open-ended. I have defined a view of the work in this book, and I have described it in process terms. I have said that humans are here to create by providing hands for the universe's creative force in the matrix of matter. We are here to answer an ultimate question the creative force asks. "How," heaven asks, "can my angelic alchemists and architects bring form to matter in ways that explore the infinite possibilities of creation and do such work without end?"

The answer seems to be that the mystery of creation has formed a matrix of matter as laboratory and created a being of curiosity suited to play in that matrix. Humans are those beings. Humans come armed with a variety of unique tools, or gifts, that might facilitate a new path of creation. Humans are a collaboration of a drop of heaven and a drop of earth—soul and body—inherently connected and connecting the elements of both earthly matter and heavenly design-intelligence. What is the process heaven has designed? It has given humans freedom of choice to follow their curious noses in a playground of possibility. And the price of playing is what we already know of art in general. If you are going to express a distinct form of created beauty that art represents, you first have to do the work of learning your craft. We have to become skillful before we can become sustainably playful. Curiosity without craft leaves us in the sandbox of childhood and vulnerable to the masters of manipulation.

So the process which cultivates the craft of exploring the creative possibilities in the matrix of matter requires that we develop the soul skill, then the body skill, that are the price of doing some serious play in the great matrix. Cultivating that skill alongside our efforts at healing moves everything along a bit faster.

At some point, I noticed that the earth matrix included some very powerful and intelligent plants. My curiosity asked, "What are these for, and what can I do with them?" Nothing, I thought, is placed in the matrix without purpose.

What I found is that the plant medicines, in *ceremonial* encounters, *sped up* the process in which I was already engaged. I was already working with an Asian process of meditation that allowed me to remove my consciousness from its enmeshment with the body. The medicine accelerated that piece of process in minutes far more than years of meditation had done. Yet, my meditation skill was absolutely necessary for me to profit from that more abrupt separation of consciousness from body. It is one thing to see that consciousness *can* separate from body. Anybody can do that with any number of substances, including television. It is quite another to develop the skill that allows intention to place the consciousness in or out of the body at will and to navigate multidimensional terrains with a novel, creative outcome. So meditation gave me skill. Plant medicine gave me opportunity to explore more broadly. Could my meditation have taken me there? Frankly, I doubt it. I have no doubt that meditation can take one's personal consciousness to the edge of oneness and dissolve it on that end of the spectrum. But meditation has not explored the depths of the earth matrix. It was a higher consciousness that suggested to me that the earth has a heart. It was the medicine that unexpectedly took me there.

Meditation has long been a heavenly science. As such, it has facilitated separating soul from body. Medicine is an earthly science. As such, it facilitates bringing the soul into the body, the body into a compatible relationship with the soul, and soul and body into relationship with the earth.

The heavenly science has courted the life force that is unique to the body. We know that life force in the context of Asian meditation traditions as the *kundalini*. It is often said that the kundalini is snakelike, coiled at the base of the spine. Much emphasis is given to the process of activating the kundalini in the Eastern traditions, but the purpose of doing so is different than using the life force of the body to serve creation. In the Eastern traditions, kundalini is used primarily to drive the consciousness upward into the heavenly realms. It works beautifully, in my own way of thinking, to separate soul from body so that soul can gain awareness of itself as an entity distinct from the body. But driving the soul upward toward a remembrance of its origin, for me, is the necessary but insufficient step taken toward becoming a co-creator in the matrix of matter. The soul needs to return to the body and return the body to the earth in order to do the work of creation.

I have said that the body, when it feels safe and has begun to release its historic trauma, will turn to the soul and fall in love. But falling in love with the soul, even if the body is ready for a more mature relationship with soul, is not a choice, so much as an infatuation of the body for the soul's outpouring of love. The body, like the soul, has a choice to make if a mature relationship is to form between soul and body. Ultimately, the body has to release enough trauma to open itself not only to the soul, but to the greater life force—life force from a more sustainable source than the stored kundalini represents. To do the work of creation takes more fuel than is necessary to blast the soul beyond body orbit and back to heaven. The work of creation requires that the body have a steady supply of life force that can only come with a continuing relationship between body and earth. Plant medicines seem to bring the body to a greater capacity to receive and run the life force. One of the most radical experiences that come with the plant medicines has been, for me at least, feeling the body expand its capacity to run life force through its relatively dense nature. What made my body tremble and shake in early ceremonies now flows far more easily in my body. Just as medicine and heavenly guides have been my allies in approaching my work on the planet, so now has the life force made itself available as ally to the work of the body serving the agenda of the soul. The body is the agent that makes the choice to access this force. The soul cannot do this for the body.

And to bring the Eastern vision of the kundalini as serpent full circle, the vision of life force that consistently presented itself to me in ceremony with the ayahuasca was that of not one serpent, but uncountable numbers of serpents covering the immediate landscape of my vision. It is as though the kundalini serpent of my body is the battery, and life force is the sun that restores it. As I have become used to seeing those serpents moving toward me in the visionary space of ceremony, my body opens with anticipation of the now familiar experience of ecstasy as their energy enters my body. And this life force, much larger than the kundalini battery of my prior experience, draws me deeper into and onto the earth, rather than propelling my soul away from it.

Can all of that be done without the medicine? I have to plead ignorance. I have already walked the medicine path and cannot now backtrack. The road forked. I took the shamanic route, but I did so with a pack of skills acquired with a meditative apprenticeship that has now matured into its own distinct craft with the flavor of that unique fusion. I have, as Don Umberto suggested, mixed and matched. So my sense is that the medicine drives the soul/body/creation process faster and deeper.

I sense now that humans as a species have been stamped with a freshness date about to expire. Individual humans have always had a freshness date, but our earth is about to empty the shelves entirely unless we refresh the stock. Time is now a much greater factor than it was before the industrial revolution, specifically because our curiosity has been diverted by greed empowered with fossil fuels and technology. Because time is a factor, faster and deeper is absolutely a serious consideration.

What do I say to my clients about using plant medicines? I tell them to do the soul work in the heart. Engage the body and flood it with love. Using the plant medicines is always a consideration, but remember that it is not a unilateral decision. When the student is ready, the teacher will appear, and it is the teacher who will decide when the student is ready. The medicine may speak to you, or it may not. Many of my fellow travelers on the medicine path have said they came in response to a felt calling. So I would say that some of us are called to the medicine. Some are not. And if not now, perhaps later. You will know. It is not for me to recommend. Work your process. Be intentional. Develop your craft. And listen with your heart. The medicines are moving across the planet quickly, and they are in the building now.

If you feel the medicines calling to you in the space of your heart, know that the calling is only a calling. I like to say that we navigate with our hearts, but we have to plot the path with the head. Heart tells us where to go; mind makes the reservations. While, and because, the medicines are becoming increasingly available across the planet, they are in the hands of entrepreneurs and charlatans who exploit our being called. I wrote about these issues at some length in my book *Soul Tribes and Tambos.*

There are only a few competent facilitators. Be careful how you choose. Even with a skilled and safe facilitator, the medicine cannot do all the work. You are better off meeting it halfway with your own skillful process, without which you cannot integrate the gifts of the medicine. In addition, the medicine does not provide the protection your body needs when the great openness comes to the body in ceremony. For that, you need facilitators who can hold space and provide protection. Some of these may have a process for integrating the gift of the plant. Many do not. And in time, you may be ready to meet the medicine directly, on your own, without an intermediary. Take care. Listen through your heart. Listen to your body. Use your head. Be skillful.

# 16

# DISCOVERING SOUL
# PURPOSE

THESE PRIOR CHAPTERS REPRESENT A rather a long journey to come to the simplicity of a process that is already built into you. You are the one you've been waiting for, as our Hopi friends have been saying for a long time. This chapter will focus on how the soul uses the body's sensuality to feel into purpose.

Linguist Noam Chomsky argued that the brain is hardwired for languages and that humans, consequently, do not have to learn language from a blank slate. In a similar way, humans are preconfigured to know their purpose. But, as with language skill, there is a process of learning that activates the capacity to know purpose. In the earlier chapters, I have described a learning pathway that leads to your inherent and natural capacity to *know*. With the skills I have described, you can know your purpose as a soul sojourning in a relatively healed body on an increasingly chaotic planet.

Your purpose will not finally yield to being described in so many words, except in a very general sense. Your general purpose is to create. At that general level, we are all programmed to create novelty—new ways to do what is necessary to do in order for humans to thrive in collaboration with a loving and nurturing planet in a continually changing cultural and physical environment—all for the general purpose of fostering creation in a sustainable way. We are following our curiosity into the future, but we have to create sustainably to get there. If we create war machines and pesticides with our beautiful intelligences, our curiosity will not take us much further.

In order to create sustainably, we have first to learn to give and receive Love. The soul's light *is* Love. But we have to bring that general level of creation to the specific and do so with a skillful focus: what will you create with Love? I have capitalized Love to distinguish the phenomenon to which I refer from the emotional attachment that most of us regard as love.

What you will create at the level of the specific depends on the gifts that your soul brings. For some of us, those gifts are apparent from early in life. For others, the gifts only become apparent in time. But the gifts don't deliver themselves. The process I describe here reveals both the gifts and their purpose. Gifts are revealed by propensity. Purpose is revealed by opportunity.

You will find that delivering your gifts into the world will require you to bring not only the focus of the soul, but intention and imagination and—there's more—a conscious *choice* to do so, empowered by personal will and determination. It requires work.

Lastly, because purpose arises in collaboration with opportunity, purpose doesn't define itself once and forever. Gifts might be forever. I had a sense when I was very young that I would be a writer. But I know now that writing is a tool. It is a tool that has become my craft, and my craft has had to be developed over time with practice. Only then does the gift mature. And the ability to express myself in this way might be a gift. But it is not my purpose.

My purpose will be revealed not in the fact *that I write,* but in *what I write,* and what I write will depend on the times, the audience, and a variety of other circumstances. It is the same with my coaching. Coaching is a tool. I have taken years and years to develop the coaching into a craft. The insights that have allowed me to develop a coaching process might be my gift. But how to deliver that gift again depends on the times, the audience, and a variety of other circumstances. How do we bring gift and purpose together?

We do so with resonance. Like vibrates with like. We search for harmony between what is rising up *in us* and what is rising up *around us* after we have developed ourselves as focused souls, learned to situate ourselves in the heart portal, developed the craft of our gifts, and done the work of healing the body that allows the body to become the instrument of the soul. We need to have brought the heart and body to a state of coherence to bring all of this work together. When we have achieved a state of coherence, then our natural ability to resonate begins to connect with other coherent fields that represent the opportunity to deliver our gifts.

So, after we have done this much work and after we have developed the habit of holding ourselves in the heart portal, *then* we can reach beyond the historic blocks of body trauma that previously disabled the body instrument. Reaching beyond, we feel into what each day presents.

One way of looking at how this works is in the distinction between fate and destiny. The universe continues to churn up opportunities to deliver our gifts amidst attractive dead ends, while cloaking opportunities. Without the skill I have described here, it is largely impossible to know which is which. Fate is our experience when we are unable to know the difference but are invited to learn the difference. In that way, fate is always an invitation to learn who we are and to develop the skills that reveal our purpose. Destiny is what we can choose to create from daily opportunities when we are skilled enough to resonate with coherent opportunities and recognize when we are resonating with incoherent circumstances to which our historic issues have attracted us, once more—circumstances that would again lead to dead ends. Our destiny is found in the coherent opportunities and the avoidance of incoherent circumstances.

The familiar *law of attraction* comes fully into play now. The universe doesn't provide us with what we want in the form we want it. It provides what we need in the form we need it. If we are unskillful, the universe will provide us with the paradoxical learning opportunity (fate) from which we can, if we pay attention, become more conscious and more skillful.

The challenge is to see that what is swirling around us includes both what we need and what we don't. Ultimately, our capacity for resonance, combined with the skill of knowing from a coherent heart with full access to the body's sensuality, brings our gifts into merger with the opportunities with which our coherence resonates. Our minds will more often than not be unable to catch and understand those connections in the moment. It may take years for the mind to understand how a particular opportunity connected with our gifts. However, the more I have been able to work this process skillfully, the more I am able to recognize both the opportunity and its potential meaning in or near to the moment. I can often feel synchronicity popping around me. The energy flow is palpable. Sometimes I can't. I have to keep focusing attention on the process. I have to continue working.

Resonance is a feeling that registers at the level of knowing. It is not a thought, although it might immediately give rise to one. For each of us, that resonance has a *signature*—a particular feeling that you will learn to recognize. For me, there is often a tingle in my body that is accompanied with a smile—a smile that responds to the sense of "aha, that's it." Increasingly, I feel a wave of joy as the resonance arises. I *know* something is afoot, that an opportunity is presenting. There is a flow. Resistance seems to diminish. I feel *drawn* to investigate. These signals are, I think, quite individual, but necessary for each of us to recognize and cultivate. Ultimately, we do so by developing the habit of holding ourselves—the self-identified and focused soul—steadily and always in the heart portal and paying attention to the responses of a relatively healed body.

Often we are presented with a choice between a couple of opportunities or choice points in our lives. The mind will tend to jump in and make its lists of pros and cons. It will analyze, compare, and rationalize. But the major decision points in our lives cannot be resolved in this way. The mind cannot grasp the future implication of such choices. But the soul based in the heart *can feel* which of the choices resonates with the body's sensuality in a way we can absolutely learn to recognize. This skill development takes time.

I have worked with clients who come for some help with such decisions. It is tempting always to meet them in their minds, which I have learned not to do. If we have worked together before, we go immediately to the massage table, go through the steps of the preliminary process, and see whether there is something in the body blocking the availability of the sensual instrument. We see what arises within. Working from there, we can work our way to what is arising without and look for the signature response of the body instrument. In time, all of us can learn to do this in the quiet spot we create for this purpose: our meditation cushion, the stillness that nature offers to us, the space we create in our walks, or however else *you* may find the place of merger that reveals resonant coherence.

I have found that my mind is far too slow to assess the changes in the world as they are happening when my need is to discover the purpose of the day that defines my work of the time. But the heart and soul work just outside of time, with a different view and a way of working that is immediate, in the soul's now.

And that now of the soul and the now of the body are the times of your life.

Best wishes on your journey. Good fishing!

# POSTSCRIPT

Body's true tale is hidden
from psychology's shallow plow.
And few, to say truth,
prefer a deeper dig.
Rooty realms and mycelial web
hold little appeal
for enlightened minds
that head for heaven,
or those who flee fear
on techno-wings,
as if that could work.
At some point,
it takes boots on the ground.

No.
Archeology's autopsy
would find body's tale
painted imperfectly
on heart's cavewall
and scratched in fissures
frozen far below the surface
of the Holy Now's usual haunt.

No words speak there,
where dark feelings crouch and shuffle
and real ghosts may stir.

Body memory is seared upon blood
and flesh and bones,
memory that creeps and seeps
like crude,
thick and black,
oozing below ordinary sight
but surfacing seldom,
unless we drill down.

Pain too oozes through fissures
in earthen bodies,
sometimes surfacing
to reveal a cry for help,
to report, perhaps,
a faint tapping on some deep wall
that fear built.
*Someone lives there still!*
pain whispers
to minds distracted from bodies.
Bones and blood live
in geological time,
a different Now
that extends back
to mitochondrial mixing,
and just beyond.
Body's Now is not
an ephemeral instant,
not a mere awakened presence,
but a lifetime of embodiment.
Many lifetimes, some say.

How to excavate what taps,
what sends pain to plea?
Who will travel down
and back in time
across the body's vast Now?
Who can see with eyes
what only bones remember?

There is a way to slice time,
a place to enter
the undermind cavern,
and light to bring there.
I have traveled there.
I have seen this.

Let us reverse myth's old tale.
Let *soul* go down and in.
Body is not hell
but home,
soul's home away from home
it crossed quantum dimensions
to inhabit
and enliven
and ride.

Let us reverse shamans' old way.
*You* be the soul that journeys
through heart and deep.
Let us shift the power.
*You* be the soul who heals,
who would heal your body.
This is the new way of healing.

Soul does not ail,
but heals.
The focused soul

is more powerful
than all the body's wounds,
when it enters gently
and with love.

Let soul recover body.
Let soul hold the body
with gentle whispers
and soothing words
and wrap body
in a womb of light.
Let soul flood body
with love alighting
from heaven and earth
until body breaks fear's walls
and invites soul in.
All the way in.
Then let soul journey
in the body's Now
to the beginning of body time.
Let soul see what lies there
and here
and there.
The wise soul knows
the mycelial web
provides lighted paths
that speed the journey.
And let mind delegate
its minstrel poet
to pair with soul,
to witness what soul unearths,
to compose a song
that tells body's tale.
Let poet's breath give voice
to mute bone.
And let a fair shaman,

if a real one may be found,
hold the rope
as these two
descend deep into dark
many times,
as many times
as it takes.
There are many wounds
to witness,
many songs to write.
Let soul journey
until all songs are sung,
until all songs become one,
one tale that body
can entrust to poets' wordcraft
so wounds and remembrance
can be transformed
into one story
removed from flesh
and blood and bone,
and brought benign
to mind.

Let that story be the body's
own lachrymatory,
a vessel for grief's tears
pulled from body's deep well
and laid to rest
with love
and fire.
Bring them up.
All the way up.
Sing those tears
at fire's altar
until blessed tears recede.

This is how body time is sliced
and bones sing.
This is how soul heals body
and body falls in love
with soul.
This is how life force returns
to fill those places
wounds have carved out,
and how soul enlists body's passion
to its purpose
and body's legs
to its work.
I have seen this.

# ACKNOWLEDGMENTS

IT IS IMPOSSIBLE TO KNOW how many streams have flowed into the river of one's life. The work of many people has informed my thinking or pointed me to experiences that have created the indigenous understandings of my own mind.

Black Eagle Sun took me into his home and sweat lodge when my emotions were bursting in my chest and the pain was too loud for anything else to be heard there. He introduced me to John Milton, who has taught a way to approach vision questing to many people.

Although I spent years reading Indian and Sufi classics, I eventually fell in love with the work of Sri Aurobindo. I think it was his work that really began to bring something of soul and heart to my mind, even though the omega point he envisioned is quite different than the more earthly destination I ultimately embraced. In the ramp-up to tackling Aurobindo's work, I was greatly aided by the publications of Swami Rama's Himalayan Institute, to which I was introduced by Usharbudha Arya, later known as Swami Veda Bharati. The gayatri mantra I learned from him has never left my tongue.

I've followed the work of Joseph Chilton Pearce since his cosmic egg-cracking days, reading those early books on the beach while my children played in the water on our vacations far from New Mexico. Pearce discovered the HeartMath Institute along the way, and we both found its research to be very important. Pearce's focus on the relationship between mother's love and brain development and his willingness to see beyond the limits of conventional scientific thinking have been a great legacy. It feels as though Mae-Wan Ho's writing has taken this work to an entirely new level. Her thinking has clearly elevated my own. Both Pearce and Ho passed this year after delivering so many gifts.

The HeartMath Institute itself continues to provide significant research which points to the primacy of the heart in guiding the intelligences. Roshi Joan Halifax pointed me to the HeartMath Institute, in addition to provoking an important personal insight regarding projection that was critical in my own healing.

Arthur M. Young, the physicist who took a little time off from his work with consciousness to invent the original Bell helicopter, provided in his writing a more clear view of the evolution of consciousness than I have found elsewhere.

There were several authors, including Marion Woodman and Leonard Shlain, who helped me to see the world through the polarity of the masculine and feminine, even though vision finally became my greater teacher in that regard. My central vision of the relationship of the feminine and masculine started in a shamanic workshop conducted by Lynn Berryhill. I had many shamanic teachers along the way. I want to acknowledge Sandra Ingerman, in particular. She embodies a spirit of curiosity that is open to evolving tradition, and her integrity is without question. I'm very grateful for every moment I have spent in her classes and in conversation with her.

More recently, Elaine Pagels's great work on the Christian-era documents discovered in 1945 had a great influence on the thinking that is reflected in this book, including the title. Thanks to Dr. Pagels for permission to quote her work so extensively.

My last-minute exchange with David Hendrickson helped to fill a hole in my thinking and the last hole in my book.

It has taken the work of healing over many years for me to see and appreciate my parents for who they were. I'm grateful for their getting food on the table, modeling the value of hard work, instilling respect for education, and continuing to be there in many supportive ways. Despite hardship, their deep sense of the importance of family resulted in a loving and mutually supportive relationship among myself and my three sisters.

Last and not least, I want to acknowledge my partner, Darlene Joy, who has shared the rigor of the Peru plant medicine adventure with me since 2011. She opened her healing work to my view, allowing me the privilege of seeing directly the gift of the medicine in someone else's process. Her support has been critical in many ways, not the least of which is the co-creation of space within which to do this radical work of discovery.

# APPENDIX

### *An Overview of the Stages*
### *of Soul Evolution*
### *from*
## The Soul's Critical Path: Waking Down to the Soul's Purpose, the Body's Power, and the Heart's Passion

My own experience suggested to me that the terrain over which the soul's trajectory travels might be sensibly divided into six parts, along with six corresponding stages of consciousness that are roughly associated with those parts. These six parts and stages constitute what I have called the critical path of the soul.

## 1. PART ONE / STAGE ONE

| Terrain of the Soul Journey | Stage of Consciousness | Perspective |
|---|---|---|
| **Part One:** The gathering place of souls intermediate between heaven and earth. | **Stage One:** The soul knows that it is a soul and consciously, if not skillfully, knows that it is called upon to choose another round on the planet. | The earth journey is the soul's opportunity to learn. |

The terrain that is Part One of the soul journey is the "place" described by Er as the meadow. In this gathering place, the nature of the soul's consciousness is that it knows itself to be a soul seeing directly through its own eyes. This is a soul perspective. Although a self-aware soul perspective, it is not necessarily a developed or mature perspective. Whatever the level of development, this is stage one consciousness.

In that self-aware state, the soul chooses a life. The Sisters imprint a fate upon that life—a fate that is not disclosed. The soul drinks from the River of Forgetting. The soul is swept away, to be born upon the earth, carrying a secret that it will keep even from itself until the skillful means of discovery of that secret has been acquired. The secret is that soul's destiny and how that destiny is embedded in the soul's fate.

## 2. PART TWO / STAGE TWO

| Terrain of the Soul Journey | Stage of Consciousness | Perspective |
|---|---|---|
| **Part Two:** The dense body field and the earth. | **Stage Two:** Attention is captured by the body, held in a provisional personality, and entrained outward by culture. The soul has lost control of the ability to control its own attention. | Life is a struggle. I (the personality) am a victim of circumstances. Things that happen to me are either good or bad. The bad is my fate. I can't control my fate or emotional reactions because those depend on what happens to me. Life is out of my control unless I outsmart it. |

Part Two of the terrain of the soul's trajectory is the body. Coming to the earth for the birth of the body represents the beginning, but not the end, of a process of merger. That merger first involves a mutual entrainment of the respective fields of the body and the soul to a degree sufficient to sustain life in the body. The further progress of this entrainment is not automatic. The initial stages of this entrainment are unconscious to the soul. Further entrainment requires skillful attention, which represents the work of the ensuing stages of consciousness at the soul level. If the soul experiences the body to be alien territory, that's because it is. And the body, similarly, may experience the soul as an invader.

This second stage of consciousness is characterized by the inability of the soul to control attention, thereby defaulting attention to culture's control of an immature personality—a default personality that reflects the stronger identification with the body, an attention directed outward, and an almost total absence of awareness of the soul. Modern culture takes advantage of that opportunity intentionally, mercilessly, and skillfully. In this environment, particularly without the presence of a nurturing connection with the earth, the surface personality often feels out of control. For the personality that arises from this preliminary merger of soul and body in a challenging environment, this is the stage of victim mentality and an engagement with the external world that excludes the inner. Dissociation, depression, and a deeply felt sense of disconnection are common as the personality finds itself unable to make sense of the world or navigate skillfully in it.

## 3. STAGE THREE / PART THREE

| Terrain of the Soul Journey | Stage of Consciousness | Perspective |
|---|---|---|
| **Part Three:** The terrain includes the body, but also includes the other dimensions beyond time/space. There is a move from the exclusively external to include the internal. | **Stage Three:** A battle for control of attention begins, with culture on one side and the nascent soul on the other. The soul is now working, even below the level of conscious awareness, to capture control of the attention that has been taken by the personality and culture during the soul's forgetfulness. | Life remains confusing even as a sense of purpose has begun to form. I begin to shift from seeing everything as good or bad to seeing what happens as *just is*. Reactivity begins to diminish as I learn to reclaim the projections that are the basis of my victim perspective. |

Part Three of the terrain has now expanded in the same way that the soul's awareness has also begun to expand. The soul is aware not only of the density of its body but also of the heaven dimensions that call out to it, helping the soul to awaken and emerge. We may feel these as awakenings—stirrings, intuitions, knowings, and peak "spiritual" experiences.

Within stage three consciousness, small awakenings may occur many times until they form the critical mass sufficient to shift from a personality perspective that excludes the soul to one that begins to contemplate the presence of the soul. Even though the ultimate work of the soul involves a full partnership with the body, with attention in the control of the soul, this preliminary part of the soul work is about remembering itself. This step carries the attention away from the body—including its thoughts, feelings, and sensory attachments—to a remembrance of the fundamental sense of connection that is the mature soul's natural state.

Like in my own near-death experience, there is a return to a consciousness of the heaven dimensions. For some religions, that return would be the end of the journey and possibly—from some perspectives—the end of a punishment that the earth journey has represented. But from the soul perspective that I am suggesting here, this gradual return to awareness of the heaven dimensions and the increasing access to "peak" experiences are only a preparation for the next stage. Stage three consciousness is about recognizing something we've known, but from a much different perspective. In that remembrance, we know heaven for the first time from the soul's perspective of being in the body. We begin to acquaint ourselves with the body from the perspective of the soul's connection to heaven. Remembering that we are souls that left heaven allows us to get to work on the question of why we left that place and came to the earth journey to work in an unfamiliar body. This remembrance may occur in a dramatic manner, as occurred for me with the near-death experience, or in the variety of ways we will discover as we begin to focus on achieving a soul perspective. With this remembrance restored firmly in the soul's consciousness, the soul is ready to move forward to the deeper work of embodiment.

In short, stage three consciousness involves the process of learning how to control attention, learning how to wrest it from the grasp of the body and culture, placing that attention in the heart-field where the soul's awareness of itself is cultivated, and, ultimately, shifting identity from the personality to the soul.

## 4. PART FOUR / STAGE FOUR

| Terrain of the Soul Journey | Stage of Consciousness | Perspective |
|---|---|---|
| **Part Four:** Anywhere that the empowered soul now directs its attention, including the body field, the other dimensions, or the soul itself. | **Stage Four:** The soul has now captured control of attention and is able to direct attention, with some effort, to itself, to the body, and to other dimensions that contain information for the soul's further journey, setting the stage for learning how to engage more deeply with each of those destinations. | Life and its challenges are neither good nor bad, nor "just is." Life's challenges are now a gift of opportunity for soul development. "I" is now characterized increasingly by my identification with soul rather than with the personality. The soul now assumes responsibility for creating a partnership with the body in the service of the emergence of soul destiny. I no longer project responsibility for my fate or destiny on everything and everyone else. I am no longer a victim. |

The peak experiences encountered during stage three consciousness now provide meaning for our day-to-day experience of life in Part Four of the journey. While the terrain of Part Three and Part Four is the same, our experience with it becomes more intentional, intense, and skillful during stage four consciousness. My landing onto the runway of my body was a second landing within the same lifetime—a second coming of the soul in a moment of awakening that begins a purposeful effort by the soul to partner with the body in service of soul's work.

This fourth part of the trajectory is less familiar in our culture, or in any culture, for that matter. Aurobindo made it his life's work to talk about its beginning and its potential for bringing consciousness to the very cells of the body, even as he acknowledged that he did not accomplish it. This is the stage to which the notion of Tantric practice—*Vajrayana*—is introduced even though its potential is explored only in stage five. In stage four consciousness, we begin to use the soul's growing control over attention to discover and engage the variety of dimensions of reality, including the fields of body, earth, heaven, fate, destiny, and the soul itself. Stage four also represents a looking back upon the prior stages as we identify and resolve the dysfunctional patterns that have blocked the soul's emergence. So stage four represents the time of healing the body-based consequences of a victim perspective and developing the skills of soul attention, both of which are necessary to power the soul toward its destiny.

## 5. PART FIVE / STAGE FIVE

| Terrain of the Soul Journey | Stage of Consciousness | Perspective |
|---|---|---|
| **Part Five:** The body is now the temporary home base of the soul as it explores the density of time/space in the context of its connection with the other-dimensional fields that provide constant support for the soul journey. | **Stage Five:** The soul's ability to focus attention grows as it goes increasingly into the other dimensions and as it explores the density of matter. The soul's control of attention is no longer simply conscious and intentional, but increasingly automatic; and, therefore, one might say, soul is becoming more *skilled*. | Life is often joyful and full of energy, yet even more challenging in new ways. The soul's work is at the edge of the evolution of consciousness through the expression of its own purpose through the power of the body and the passion of the heart. I identify both with the whole of consciousness and with my particular soul role as a co-creator of the play of consciousness. |

The terrain remains cosmic, including every possible field that soul consciousness can visit, but the focus is upon deepening the soul's relationship with the body and earth, which is the frontier of human consciousness. We have called the stage that follows death the frontier, but that is only because we have failed to see the frontier that lies more immediately before us in this lifetime. The death stage is well traveled, but the exploration of the body/earth fields by a soul fully grounded in the heart with skillful control of attention is the very definition of the frontier of human consciousness. This is the exploration that we have come to do. We cannot leapfrog over the earlier stages and start our work here. We must all pay our dues and gain admission to stage five by working through the prior stages.

## 6. PART SIX / STAGE SIX

| Terrain of the Soul Journey | Stage of Consciousness | Perspective |
|---|---|---|
| **Part Six:** The bridge between body and the heaven dimensions that forms upon the death of the body. | **Stage Six:** If the soul has managed to control attention, then this is a direct and smooth transition. If the soul remains in stage two or three consciousness, the transition is more complex because of the personality's confusion about the process of death. | Death is a transition back to a self-aware soul state, although that remembrance may not occur immediately, and a soul confusion that occurs during life may persist for some time beyond death. |

Part Six terrain is the short bridge to the heaven dimensions, to which we journey upon death without prospect of return to this body. Stage six consciousness is a wide-awake approach to the transition of dying. All of our preparation for this transition occurs in earlier stages of consciousness as the skill of attention and the experience of using it develop and mature. That maturation may define our ability to focus attention into the death transition itself. Without that preparation, a transition from body to the heaven dimensions will occur, but it may occur in the midst of an earlier stage of consciousness. Many people experience this transition from a consciousness that is characterized by stage two consciousness, a lucky few in stage three, fewer in stage four, and a smaller number in stage five. I suspect, from my reading and the felt sense that is emerging in me, that coming to stage six from stage five may present other opportunities, but that is beyond the scope of this book.

*A Visual Schematic of the Soul Journey*

In short, the potential of this journey is that we jump "down" from heaven, hopefully recover from the fall, do the work of waking up, by which we find our way "upward" to the experience that refreshes the memory that we came from heaven on purpose, do some wide-ranging healing and practice with our newly growing soul consciousness, then focus that awakening consciousness back down into the body and the density of matter as far as we can with the help of the other-dimensional fields (frequency encoded with information), all before the soul leaves the body and returns to heaven—a down, then an up, then another down before the last up, when the body dies. A picture of that trajectory might look like this (the numbers refer to the six stages of consciousness):

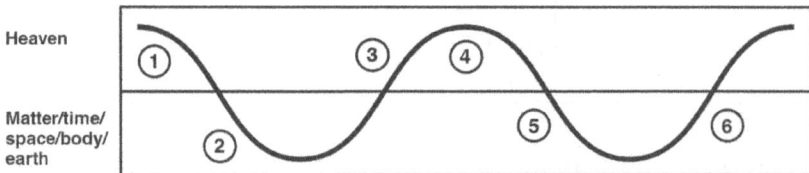

Associating labels with a line drawing doesn't give you a meaningful experience. Nevertheless, these conceptual tools help to organize what is otherwise chaotic and constantly moving information into a framework that may be helpful until your own internal territory is familiar and your movement within it becomes increasingly intuitive. The linear map helps a linear mind—and we need that linear mind even if it's a mistake to let it rule our lives—to chart some progress over longer time frames than a moment or a day. More importantly, it may help the linear mind open to a partnership with the soul through the heart.

Although it may be helpful to have a kind of rough visual of this up-and-down process divided into parts and stages, such a schematic is far too simplistic and linear to be an accurate representation of the progression of the soul in a day-to-day way. It is, after all, only a map; it is not the territory. And even though the map shows an idealized trajectory in the form of a critical path, we sometimes stand still, hesitate, go backwards or sideways, and forget what we are up to. Even if I am living mostly in stage four, I may spend a particularly difficult week in stage two until my partner reminds me that I have regressed.

None of us is completely in Part Two/stage two to the exclusion of Part Three/ stage three. Within each stage, there is a beginning, middle, and emergence into the beginning of the next. When I speak of being in one stage or another, it is really more accurate to say that the stage represents the nature of challenges with which our consciousness is faced at a particular time. To say that we are in a particular stage of consciousness is simply to say that a particular form of identity and relationship with attention is a predominant, though not exclusive, state of consciousness at a particular point in time. We routinely go back and forth between stages in particular moments, but the trend—if we persist—is to move in an arc that has identifiable benchmarks, such as the parts and stages that I am identifying here.

The signs I'm posting along the way—*parts* and *stages*—are ways of marking the milestones on the journey by saying "this is different than that," "there's a direction to the journey," and "there's a purpose embedded in this experience." Noting milestones allows us to mark a position or sense a movement and understand that something a little different is significant even if it is subtle. If we were talking about a roadmap laid out on the geography of the earth, it would be easier to see. It's more challenging to talk about consciousness. The tools are metaphor and similes, feelings, experiences, knowings, and partial understandings that we abandon when we get better understandings—much tougher territory to navigate than learning math or driving the interstate.

Our ultimate spiritual work on this journey is to get soul consciousness into the body and become the agents of consciousness through which heaven collaborates with earth to co-create at the edge of the evolution of consciousness itself. The challenge is not merely to experience consciousness beyond the body in the heaven dimensions, but to bring it into the body and to experience it fully there—here, now. No one knows where that process will lead. That is both its delight and its challenge. There may be spiritual work beyond this journey, but we probably won't know what that is until we have lived this one out.

# NOTES

1 *Gospel of Thomas,* translated by George MacRae, quoted by Elaine Pagels, in *Beyond Belief* (New York: Random House, 2003), 32.

2 Mae-Wan Ho, *The Rainbow and the Worm: The Physics of Organisms*, 3rd ed. (Singapore: World Scientific, 2008), 210.

3 Ibid., 139.

4 Ibid., 179.

5 Ibid., 180.

6 Ibid., 209.

7 The HeartMath Institute has numerous publications, most all of which cite this basic information about the heart. A good initial resource for accessing a summary of HeartMath's research is one of its websites: www.heartmath. org.

8 Ho, *The Rainbow and the Worm,* 180.

9 Ibid., 195.

10 Ibid., 203.

11 Ibid., 217.

12 Ibid., 222.

13 Ibid., 228.

14 Ibid., 236.

15 Ibid., 237-239.

16 Ibid., 279.

17  Ibid.. 293.

18  Ibid., 315.

19  Joseph Chilton Pearce, *The Heart-Brain Matrix: How the Heart Can Teach the Mind New Ways to Think* (Rochester, VT: Park Street Press, 2012), Kindle version, location 703 of 3599.

20  Ibid., location 2401.

21  Ibid., location 2911.

22  Ho, *The Rainbow and the Worm,* 314-315.

23  Elaine Pagels, *The Gnostic Gospels* (New York: Vintage Books, 1981) (hereafter cited as GG); Elaine Pagels, *Adam, Eve, and the Serpent* (New York: Random House, 1988) (hereafter cited as AES); and Elaine Pagels, *Beyond Belief: The Secret Gospel of Thomas* (New York: Random House, 2005) (hereafter cited as BB).

24  Pagels, BB, 15.

25  Ibid., 6.

26  Ibid., 27.

27  Ibid., 11.

28  Ibid., 7.

29  Ibid., 7-8.

30  Ibid., 28-29.

31  Ibid., 54.

32  Ibid., 33-34.

33  Pagels, GG, xxxviii.

34  Pagels, BB, 57-58.

35  Ibid., 150.

36  Ibid., 45.

37  Ibid., 45.

38  Ibid., 46.

39  Ibid., 67.

40  Ibid., 60.

41  Ibid., 75.

42  Ibid., 164.

43  Pagels, GG, 27.

44  Ibid., 26.

45  Ibid., 29-30.

46  Ibid., 43-44.

47  Ibid., 59.

48  Pagels, BB, 130-131.

49  Ibid., 133.

50  Ibid., 136-138.

51  Pagels, GG, 161.

52  Ibid., 162-164.

53  Ibid., 169.

54  Ibid., 45, 47.

55  Ibid., xv.

56  Ibid., xvii.

57  Ibid., xxiii-xxiv.

58  Pagels, BB, 157.

59  Ibid., 168.

60  Ibid., 169.

61  Ibid., 170.

62  Ibid., 171.

63  Ibid., 170-171.

64  Ibid., 173-174.

65  Ibid., 174.

66  Ibid., 97.

67  Ibid., 178.

68  Ibid., 180.

69  Pagels, AES, xxv-xxvi.

70  Ibid., 112-113.

71  Ibid., 124-125.

72  Ibid., 133.

73  Ibid., 150.

74  Pagels, BB, 183-184.

75  Ibid., 28-29, 183.

76  Pagels, GG, 181.

77  Ibid., 171.

78  Ibid., 172-73.

79  Ibid., 173-174.

80  Ibid., 22.

81  Ibid., 174.

82  Ibid., 176.

83  Ibid., 176.

84  Ibid., 7.

85  Ibid., 12.

86  Ibid., 12.

87  Ibid., 13.

88  Ibid., 23.

89  Pagels, BB, 104-105.

90  Edward S. Herman and Noam Chomsky, *Manufacturing Consent: The Political Economy of the Mass Media* (New York: Pantheon Books, 1988), 306.

91  Andrew Bacevich, *America's War for the Greater Middle East: A Military History* (New York: Random House, 2016).

92  Interview of Andrew Bacevich, by Patrick L. Smith, Salon (Salon.com), May 15, 2016: "The scope of our failure: The real story of our decades-long foreign policy disaster that set the Middle East on fire."

93  Bacevich, *America's War*, 361-362.

94  Ibid., 363-365.

95  Ibid., 368-369.

96  Interview of Bacevich.

97  David C. Hendrickson, "The Republic in Peril: American Empire and the Liberal Tradition," unpublished manuscript, and email communication with author, May 18, 2016.

98  David C. Hendrickson, email communication with author, June 27, 2016.

99  Pearce, *The Heart-Mind Matrix*, Kindle version, location 1896.

# ABOUT THE AUTHOR

JOHN P. DAVIDSON coaches souls, writes about souls, and teaches related workshops. He lives in the United States and travels to Peru. Information about his work and other books may be found at www.soulscriticalpath.com.